FREE TECHNOLOGY FOR
LIBRARIES

Library Technology Essentials

About the Series

The **Library Technology Essentials** series helps librarians utilize today's hottest new technologies as well as ready themselves for tomorrow's. The series features titles that cover the A–Z of how to leverage the latest and most cutting-edge technologies and trends to deliver new library services.

Today's forward-thinking libraries are responding to changes in information consumption, new technological advancements, and growing user expectations by devising groundbreaking ways to remain relevant in a rapidly changing digital world. This collection of primers guides libraries along the path to innovation through step-by-step instruction. Written by the field's top experts, these handbooks serve as the ultimate gateway to the newest and most promising emerging technology trends. Filled with practical advice and projects for libraries to implement right now, these books inspire readers to start leveraging these new techniques and tools today.

About the Series Editor

Ellyssa Kroski is the Director of Information Technology at the New York Law Institute as well as an award-winning editor and author of 22 books including *Law Librarianship in the Digital Age* for which she won the AALL's 2014 Joseph L. Andrews Legal Literature Award. Her ten-book technology series, The Tech Set, won the ALA's Best Book in Library Literature Award in 2011. She is a librarian, an adjunct faculty member at Pratt Institute, and an international conference speaker. She speaks at several conferences a year, mainly about new tech trends, digital strategy, and libraries.

Titles in the Series

FREE TECHNOLOGY FOR LIBRARIES

Amy Deschenes

ROWMAN & LITTLEFIELD
Lanham • Boulder • New York • London

Published by Rowman & Littlefield
A wholly owned subsidiary of The Rowman & Littlefield Publishing Group,
Inc.
4501 Forbes Boulevard, Suite 200, Lanham, Maryland 20706
www.rowman.com

Unit A, Whitacre Mews, 26-34 Stannary Street, London SE11 4AB

British Library Cataloguing in Publication Information Available

Library of Congress Cataloging-in-Publication Data

Deschenes, Amy, 1984–
Free technology for libraries / Amy Deschenes.
pages cm. – (Library technology essentials ; 3)
Includes bibliographical references and index.
ISBN 978-1-4422-5296-7 (cloth : alk. paper) – ISBN 978-1-4422-5297-4 (pbk. : alk. paper) – ISBN
978-1-4422-5928-7 (ebook).
Libraries–Information technology. I. Title.
Z678.9.D45 2015
025.00285–dc23
2015011510

∞ ™ The paper used in this publication meets the minimum requirements of
American National Standard for Information Sciences Permanence of Paper
for Printed Library Materials, ANSI/NISO Z39.48-1992.

Printed in the United States of America

To my mother and grandmother, who took me to the library.

CONTENTS

SERIES EDITOR'S FOREWORD

Free Technology for Libraries is an all-in-one passport to today's best free technologies that can be used in libraries for outreach and events, resource management, and even web development. The authority on free library technology, Amy Deschenes gives a complete overview of what options libraries have available to them for managing internal documentation, reference statistics, purchase requests, and more. This outstanding, practical volume guides the reader through how to implement a scalable e-resources management system, how to use screen sharing for remote reference, how to create an HTML5 Responsive website with no design experience, and much more.

The idea for the Library Technology Essentials book series came about because there have been many drastic changes in information consumption, new technological advancements, and growing user expectations over the past few years to which forward-thinking libraries are responding by devising groundbreaking ways to remain relevant in a rapidly changing digital world. I saw a need for a practical set of guidebooks that libraries could use to inform themselves about how to stay on the cutting edge by implementing new programs, services, and technologies to match their patrons' expectations.

Libraries today are embracing new and emerging technologies, transforming themselves into community hubs and places of cocreation through makerspaces, developing information commons spaces, and even taking on new roles and formats, all the while searching for ways to decrease budget lines, add value, and prove the ROI (return on investment) of the library. The Library Technology Essentials series is a collection of primers to guide libraries along the path to innovation through step-by-step instruction. Written by the field's top experts, these handbooks are meant to serve as the ultimate gateway to the newest and most promising emerging technology trends. Filled with practical advice and project ideas for libraries to implement right now, these books will hopefully inspire readers to start leveraging these new techniques and tools today.

Each book follows the same format and outline, guiding the reader through the A–Z of how to leverage the latest and most cutting-edge technologies and trends to deliver new library services. The "Projects" chapters comprise the largest portion of the books, providing library initiatives that can be implemented by both beginner and advanced readers accommodating for all audiences and levels of technical expertise. These projects and programs range from the basic "How to Circulate Wearable Technology in Your Library" and "How to Host a FIRST Robotics Team at the Library" to intermediates such as "How to Create a Hands-Free Digital Exhibit Showcase with Microsoft Kinect" and the more advanced options such as "Implementing a Scalable E-Resources Management System" and "How to Gamify Library Orientation for Patrons with a Top Down Video Game." Readers of all skill levels will find something of interest in these books.

Amy Deschenes is the user experience specialist for Harvard Library and former systems and web applications librarian at Simmons College Library in Boston. She has been writing and presenting about emerging technologies and libraries for many years now, so I knew that she would be the perfect author for this book. And she far surpassed my expectations that I had for this title. Amy's knowledge and expertise shine through in this exceptional book that is at once innovative and easy to read. If you want to learn all there is to know about adopting free technology in your library from start to finish, this is the book for you.

—Ellyssa Kroski
Director of Information Technology
New York Law Institute
http://www.ellyssakroski.com
http://ccgclibraries.com
ellyssakroski@yahoo.com

PREFACE

Free Technology for Libraries sounds like an overwhelming topic, but this book will serve as your guide when navigating the array of free applications and tools available online. Some of them you are probably already familiar with in your personal life, and some are specific to libraries. Because there is a dizzying amount of choices when it comes to free and open-source software, you'll need some strategies to figure out where best to spend your time and effort in order to adopt the right tools for your library's needs. This book offers practical information on free technology for both those new to library technology and more seasoned professionals. Reading this book will give you strategies for deciding when free tools are a better choice than proprietary and tips on how to implement them successfully.

ORGANIZATION AND AUDIENCE

This concise handbook is chock-full of everything you need to get started with free and open-source technology solutions in your library. It is organized in seven chapters. Chapter 1 provides helpful background information that will get you in the right mindset for exploring the free technologies detailed in this book. There is also a list of some common terms you should be familiar with before diving in and tips on some of the core skills you will need in order to support the majority of free technology applications. Chapter 2 recommends some great library technology resources to peruse for ideas, as well as a straightforward process for evaluating new technology. Chapter 3 describes, in detail, a variety of free technology applications that are available and how they might be used in a library setting. The technologies are organized into two categories: outreach and events, and resource management and web development. Chapter 4 is where you'll find in-depth case studies, interviews, and examples of how all types of libraries are using some of the free tools discussed in chapter 3. Take inspiration from the librarians in this section, and consider how you might adopt similar strategies at your library. In chapter 5, there are in-depth, step-by-step projects outlined for you. Following the directions in this chapter will guide you through implementations such as the following: set up a basic WordPress site, create great e-mail marketing campaigns with MailChimp, and manage e-resources metadata with CORAL. Chapter 6 features some handy and brief tips for setting up and maintaining free tech. In chapter 7, we'll have a look at some future trends in free technology for libraries. Finally, you'll find some great recommended reading suggestions to provide you with even more ideas.

ACKNOWLEDGMENTS

I was invited to write this book by Ellyssa Kroski, based on my various professional presentations she had seen. I could not have finished the book without her guidance, thoughtful questions, and coaching.

My sincerest thanks to the creative and knowledgeable librarians who agreed to provide details about their own adventures with free library tech projects for the case studies included in this book. I'm sure you'll be inspired by their experiences.

I am tremendously thankful for my wonderful family, friends, and colleagues at Simmons College for their support, interest, and encouragement in my little book. And a very special thanks to Brendan, for always telling me to "go for it."

I

AN INTRODUCTION TO FREE TECHNOLOGY

"Do more with less." "Reduce costs." "Rethink our budget." These phrases probably sound familiar if you work in a library. All types of libraries continue to face financial restrictions due to funding cuts, changes in communities, and the needs of the public. In the past the library may have been able to purchase a new technology tool for enhancing services or managing resources, but now there is less money to spend on these endeavors. However, a lack of funding does not have to prevent the implementation of top-notch technology systems and tools that can solve all kinds of problems.

There are a plethora of free technology tools and applications available to libraries, and it can be daunting to select which is the right solution for your organization's needs. Although it is tempting to implement the newest, most exciting tools out there, especially when they're free, creating a plan for when and how to use free tools will make the adoption of free technology solutions much simpler. It's easy to say, "We're going to try using Google Drive," and then end up with some staff using it to collaborate on documents, while others upload various file types and share those, and still others decide to keep using Microsoft Office. Creating a clear plan with specific goals will make the implementation of free technology tools much easier.

Before setting up a new free technology tool, ask yourself, your colleagues, and your supervisor these kinds of questions: What problem are we trying to solve? Does this system solve it? Are there other options that might be better? Rather than leading with the *product*, lead with the *problem*. A discussion that includes these kinds of questions will most likely lead to a clear plan with specific goals. For example,

> **Problem:** We need a way to easily collaborate on documentation in real time with staff in various branch locations.
> **Solution:** Adopt Google Drive as a collaboration tool for documents that require input from multiple stakeholders.

There would need to be a detailed action plan, guidelines for use, and training provided to staff, but this approach puts the problem at the forefront of the plan, instead of the technology. This approach allows for the gradual introduction of a new technology to the staff and patrons as a response to a problem or goal, rather than simply because it is free.

THE REAL TRUTH: "FREE" ISN'T ACTUALLY FREE

Wait, what? You told me I could implement these projects for free! While it is true the solutions discussed in this book are available for no monetary cost, there are other resources that will be required to support them and can include things like physical hardware, staff time, and training. However, your library might already have these resources—and even if you don't they are available at a *minimal* cost.

Every time you implement a free technology in your library, you will need staff time to set up, maintain, and enhance each of these solutions. Ask yourself (and your staff), Do we have the staff bandwidth and knowledge to effectively support this technology? If you have someone on your staff who is familiar with PHP (a scripting language) and MySQL (a database) or is willing and has time to learn, then a self-hosted, open-source web application might work for your library. However, if your staff bandwidth is low, you might consider using an out-of-the-box solution, meaning there is minimal technical know-how involved to support the solution. Even free technology requires some amount of maintenance such as installing upgrades, adjusting to system redesigns, and updating content. It is important to have these discussions about staff support and make these kinds of decisions before implementing a free technology tool.

Another consideration that might have some associated cost is the infrastructure for supporting these free technologies. With some of the solutions discussed in this book, you will need a web server to host the software. Your library may already have a web server in place, or you may need to purchase server space from a hosting company. Often this service can be obtained for less than one hundred dollars annually and is completely managed by the vendor. If this isn't a cost your library can absorb, don't worry! There are many projects and tools discussed in this book that don't require any external infrastructure to set up.

LEARN THE LINGO: TYPES OF FREE TECHNOLOGY

Before we dive into the wonderful plethora of free technology available to solve your library problems, let's define some terms for clarity and understanding.

Web application. An application that is completely hosted online and managed via a web browser. Users usually need to sign up for an account using an e-mail address. Some examples of web applications discussed in this book include Google Drive, MailChimp, and Zoho Creator.

Open-source application. An application that is downloaded from the Internet and installed on your own web server or computer. Open-source applications are often, though not always, free. You can modify the source code, hence the name "open" source. An example of an open-source application discussed in this book is CORAL ERMS.

Hosting service versus *dedicated local web server*

- *Hosting service.* This is a subscription service wherein you essentially "rent" web space from a hosting company. You can use this web space to set up a website or open-source application by uploading web files. You will also need to register a domain name in order to create your library URL such as openlibrary.org.
- *Dedicated local server.* This is a physical server you support yourself. A server is a computer that manages access to a shared resource (like an open-source application). You can buy a physical server or purchase access to a virtual server from a service like

Amazon VPC. If you configure the server as a web server, you can upload web files and host a website or open-source application.

Domain name. Your website's address. You need to purchase this from a company that sells domain names. Often you can purchase a domain name as an add-on to a hosting service. You may only purchase domain names that are not taken by other members of the public. If your library has a website already, you may be able to use a subfolder of the existing domain (e.g., http://www.simmons.edu/library/archives). In this example "www.simmons.edu" is the domain and /library/archives are folders under the domain. Otherwise you'll need to purchase a domain name if you wanted to create an original address such as www.simmonscollegearchives.com.

Source code and *client-side library*

- *Source code* is the code you download that contains the "guts" of the program. For example, in the HTML5 Template project, you will download the source code for the template that can be customized with your own content.
- *Client-side library* is a set of codes, usually JavaScript, that you can download in order to build a certain kind of web application. Basically, these client-side libraries contain handy shortcuts for easier JavaScript development. In this book we'll look at Sheets-ee.js for displaying data from a Google Spreadsheet on your website. Other client-side libraries you may have heard of include jQuery (used for website manipulation) and D3.js (used for chart building).

HELPFUL TECHNOLOGIES TO KNOW

You can certainly implement most of the tools discussed in this book without any or with very minimal technology skills, but if you're looking to develop some of your own technical know-how while implementing free tools, here are the skills that will get you through the majority of projects listed in this book. If none of these are familiar to you, that is no problem! Many of the tools don't require any specialized knowledge, but if you want to do some deeper customization and really dig in, these are the skills to develop.

- *HTML/HTML5*. The markup language used to create websites.
- *CSS*. A styling language used to format HTML and XML documents.
- *MySQL*. An open-source, relational database.
- *PHP*. A scripting language used to develop websites. It is often used as the connector language between an HTML document and a MySQL database.

If you want to learn more about any of the above skill sets, there are free online tools out there you can take advantage of. These sites offer quality documentation and some offer hands-on tutorials that provide you with a great foundation.

Learning HTML and CSS

- Codecademy | www.codecademy.com
- CodeSchool | www.codeschool.com
- HTMLDog | http://htmldog.com

Learning MySQL and PHP

- Free Web Master Help | www.freewebmasterhelp.com
- Udemy Course (video lectures) | www.udemy.com

I'M READY TO START! HOW TO USE THIS BOOK

This book was written for a wide variety of library professionals. If you're a technology newbie and want to soak up as much as possible, I recommend perusing each section to learn about all of the free technology solutions available to and appropriate for libraries. This book is by no means an exhaustive list, but it does contain many of the most popular and user-friendly free technology tools available on the web.

There are many real-world examples of how to use these free technology tools, but all can be adapted (with a few simple tweaks) to suit your particular library. If you're a bit more advanced and feel ready to jump into some real-world scenarios, you might want to dive into the case studies and project sections. They will present detailed examples of how libraries are using these free technology solutions and step-by-step instructions for implementing them at your institution. Let's get started by looking at how to find and evaluate free technology tools.

2

GETTING STARTED WITH FREE TECHNOLOGY

The Internet offers a seemingly endless assortment of free technology tools to make your library more efficient and automate an array of processes. There are plenty of free downloads that will help your library increase productivity, build websites, create marketing materials, and organize information. It can be a challenging and overwhelming task to find and wade through these free options. However, there are some great resources that can help you through the process of determining which free technology tools are right for your library. It is also important to consider your patron needs, organizational culture, and staffing availability to determine when and which free solutions are appropriate.

FINDING FREE TECHNOLOGY TOOLS

Keeping up with free library technology can be challenging. It can be a daunting task to stay abreast of new technology trends through blogs, books, articles, podcasts, and conference proceedings. Creating a regular review strategy for yourself helps keep your research focused so you are up to date with trends in libraries and the technology world. Try using a news aggregator tool or app, such as Feedly (http://www.feedly. com/), for subscribing to blogs and websites that are regularly updated with postings about free technology tools. Here are some of the best online sites and blogs for discovering free technology tools for libraries.

Best Site for Instruction, Collaboration, and Outreach Tools

Free Technology for Teachers | Richard Byrne | www. freetech4teachers.com

Even though the primary audience for this site is teaching professionals, there is a plethora of great, free technology available for teaching workshops, information literacy instruction, and general outreach. Richard Byrne reviews tools and suggests how to use them in a classroom setting. He writes in-depth how-to articles about some especially popular tools, such as Google Docs, highlighting certain features that are especially helpful in teaching. The site focuses primarily on apps, websites, and web applications.

Best Site for Thoughtful Reflections on Libraries and Technology

Information Wants to Be Free | Meredith G. Farkas | http:// meredith.wolfwater.com/wordpress

The focus of this blog isn't a "technology site," proper, but the writing often mentions excellent free tools or open-source initiatives that are worth exploring. Meredith Farkas is a librarian at Portland Community College in Oregon and writes about everything from assessment techniques to best practices for library instruction. She is also an excellent presenter; check out her presentation "Free and Cheap Technologies to Supercharge Your Teaching" on her blog for plenty of fantastic ideas.

Best Site If You're Excited about Open-Source Software

Free/Open-Source Software for Libraries | LYRASIS | http:// foss4lib.org

Want the lowdown on the latest open-source releases for libraries? FOSS4Lib is the best place to stay up to date with the world of open-source software in libraries. You'll be able to find direct links to software downloads, along with profiles of different products. FOSS4Lib also offers an entire section devoted to decision-support tools. These tools include guides to selecting a discovery platform, to estimating the cost of open-source software, and on how to work with your parent organization on implementing and maintaining open-source software.

Best Site If You're Overwhelmed and Aren't Sure Where to Start

TechSoup for Libraries | www.techsoup.org

TechSoup is a fantastic community for libraries and nonprofits to learn about technology best practices, building a technology plan, and evaluating free tools. There are numerous how-to articles and a regularly updated blog with technology news related to libraries. There is also a wealth of information on funding sources for public libraries and support for composing grant proposals and applications. The site even includes an index of "Free Apps and Downloads" that cover areas such as office productivity, audio and video, and infrastructure.

In addition to keeping up with online postings, it can be helpful to review conference presentations, lightning rounds, and the professional literature regularly. If you're faced with a problem that you suspect a free technology tool might fix, you might search listserv archives to see if anyone has posed this question to a community like LITA, Code4Lib, or Web4Lib. You can also find free conference proceedings from the American Library Association (ALA), the Association of College and Research Libraries (ACRL), Code4Lib, Computers in Libraries, and Internet Librarian. If you attend a conference, check out a technology-focused lightning round to learn how other organizations are making use of free tools. For more information on other resources, check out the recommended reading chapter.

EVALUATING FREE TOOLS

Using the resources above you should be able to find many, many free technology tools that sound like fantastic solutions to problems your library has. It is important to not become dazzled by the possibilities of these free technology tools. The first step in implementing any technology is to start with a problem or identified need. If someone suggests the library needs to start using Join.Me for online reference appointments because it is "totally awesome and wicked cool," that may be a great suggestion. However, if you dissect that suggestion, it points to a larger identified need of the library for a tool for online screen sharing and collaboration.

Perhaps Join.Me is indeed the best solution for your library, but how would you know until you consider your own environment and what other tools exist to manage online meetings? It might be that your library already has a tool that can host online meetings, but there hasn't been enough promotion or training offered. It's also possible there might be another tool that solves this problem along with other related problems. Or there might be a tool that extends software the library already uses that is capable of facilitating online meetings. If you're the one selecting and implementing new technologies for the library, you need to develop a way to identify the requirements for identified needs and then compare the tools that are available to address this need. There are three steps to evaluate free tools:

1. Perform an *internal scan* of technology and skills.
2. Perform an *external scan* of free solutions available.
3. Determine which tool best meets the needs of your library based on the findings of the internal and external scans.

Step 1: Perform an Internal Scan

When you perform an internal scan, you want to ask yourself what your library already uses and if there is a possibility to adapt one of these tools for the identified need. A great way to do this is to examine the inventory of the software programs, applications, and websites your library already makes use of. If you don't have an inventory of the applications your library uses, create one! It will be an essential tool to keep your library's technology organized and will help you understand the impact any additions might make.

If there is nothing your library currently uses that can address the problem that needs to be solved, you'll need to see if you can find a free technology tool that can be the solution. Before you start Googling furiously, take a step back and think about your internal environment again. You've already checked your inventory of software; what about hardware? Do you have web space where you can install a web application? How much storage do you have available for an online platform? Consider what you have to support the free tools you'll want to implement.

In addition, also take into account your own skills and any other staff skills that might help support this free technology. Are you (or another staff member) familiar with HTML and CSS, JavaScript, MySQL, or PHP? Is there an opportunity for free training to learn the skills you might need for implementing a free tool? Also, make sure you are honest with yourself and any stakeholders about the amount of time a new free technology will take to implement and support. Consider asking for temporary support if the initial implementation will take more effort than the ongoing support. Taking these local considerations into account will help make the adoption, introduction, and support of the new tool easier.

Step 2: Perform an External Scan

Now that you have a good understanding of what your library has already in terms of technology and staff skills, and have determined you don't currently have something that can address the problem identified, it's time to start searching for a freely available technology solution. The obvious place to start is Google to see what's out there. A few other websites, in addition to the library-specific sites listed earlier in the chapter, are Lifehacker (http://lifehacker.com; check out their "High Five" features for solutions both free and paid for common productivity tools contributed by readers); TechCrunch (http://techcrunch.com); and TheNextWeb (http://thenextweb.com). Try searching Google for "best free [name of the tool you're looking for]" to find some ideas as well.

After researching your needs, you'll probably have a list of several options, but you'll also want to see if other libraries are using it or if there is a free tool specific to libraries that you didn't find in the typical Google search results. Now is the time to check out the websites listed earlier in the chapter and search through archives of library technology listservs such as Code4Lib (https://listserv.nd.edu), Web4Lib (https://listserv.nd.edu), and LITA (http://lists.ala.org). If you have access to a library science database, such as LIS Source or LIS Abstracts, this can also be a fantastic place to search. If you don't have access to library and information science (LIS) databases, try searching Google Scholar. Even with only a citation you might be able to get an article from your local public library's interlibrary loan service.

The last item to consider in your external scan before the decision-making process is the amount of external support available for the solutions you're considering. External support may vary from product to product. Consider the following criteria when evaluating external support:

- How detailed is the documentation?
- Is there a website containing support documentation? How often is it updated?
- Is there a support phone number, e-mail address, or other contact person?
- Is there a community of users collaborating on an e-mail list or discussion board to help troubleshoot problems?

Consider the quality, timeliness, and completeness of the documentation to understand if it will provide enough support for you with this new free technology tool.

Step 3: Determine Which Tool Best Fits Your Needs

Based on your scans, determine what system is the "best fit" for your organization. Look at all the information you've collected as a whole, including

- the stated problem or need;
- the internal scan of technology and available skills; and

- the external scan of available free technology tools, library adoption, and support documentation/community.

A good technique is to write up a proposal or requirements document that summarizes your findings to support the selection of the tool you're recommending for adoption. This proposal will articulate why the system is a good solution for your organization. Taking these steps might seem like a labor-intensive process, but once you've established the internal scan, you'll have that for future projects, and performing the external research becomes easier once you've done it a few times. Following these steps will help ensure your organization isn't adopting free tools for the sake of trends or implementing software that can't be supported with existing resources.

RISKS AND CONCERNS

You can't plan for everything. Free tools can be taken off line or discontinued, just like their paid counterparts. A great example of this is Google Reader. Google Reader was a popular free RSS feed aggregator that launched in 2005 and was retired in 2013, even though there were still many active, heavy users. Users were given a few months' notice to export their data and find a different platform to use as their RSS feed reader. If you don't remember Google Reader, just imagine being told that Gmail or Facebook were shutting down forever and you would have to go find your own alternatives. That is the level of frustration and anxiety people expressed over losing Google Reader.

The important part of the Google Reader example is that users were able to export their data from the system; when considering free tools keep this in mind. If the system has users create data, what happens to that data once you stop using the system? Is there a way to export information from the system in a common file format such as CSV (comma separated value) or SQL (structured query language)? Otherwise, if you're unable to get your data out of the old system, you'll be re-creating everything from scratch on a future platform.

Another consideration is the details of the user agreement for whichever free technology tool you're using. Make sure to read through the user agreement and consider if there are any limitations on what you can do with the software. Things to look out for include

- the amount of data you can store in the system;
- privacy of whatever data you might be storing in the system;
- the number of user accounts you can have; and
- the system features you're able to use.

These limitations might not deter you from using the free tool, but it's important to be aware of the exact functionality you'll be able to take advantage of. If there is a feature you're interested in that's only available in the paid version of a tool, it might be worthwhile to "pilot" the tool using the free version and then consider if upgrading to the paid version would be possible. You might also want to combine the use of multiple, smaller free tools instead of paying for a comprehensive paid solution (see the case study on using Jing and ScreenMarker together).

3

TOOLS AND APPLICATIONS

Now that you have a handle on the basics of what to look for when considering free technology, let's dive a bit deeper into some specific applications that can be useful for libraries. Each of these tools has been used successfully in libraries in different ways. We'll look at specific library examples and detailed projects involving these tools in chapters 4 and 5. This chapter will give you a strong understanding of the variety of tools that are available for free and what features they offer. We will look at applications that can be used for outreach and events, as well as those more appropriate for resource management and web design.

TOOLS FOR OUTREACH AND EVENTS

Libraries can use free technology tools to facilitate online teaching, host virtual programming, or conduct web-based research appointments. There are many tools available for this type of collaboration that allow the staff to set up group meetings, video chat, and screen sharing. Each of the tools in this section provides the ability to host one or more of these activities. Consider what your organization's goals are before deciding if one of these tools is the right fit. The more basic tools are listed first, followed by more complex tools.

ScreenMarker

ScreenMarker is a software download that allows you to make markings on your screen in real time. This tool is extremely helpful for presentations or creating how-to videos to demonstrate certain functionality. The software needs to be downloaded and launched; no installation is required, so you are even able to use it on a public computer where you might not have the ability to install software. Once the software is launched, you will see a toolbar that allows you to highlight, circle, draw, and write on any part of your screen. Use it similar to how you might use a laser pointer, to draw attention to certain parts of the screen. The markings can then be cleared using the eraser tool. This tool is fantastic to use in conjunction with the other screen-sharing and virtual-meeting tools described in this section.

Jing

Have you ever wanted to create an annotated screenshot or quick video to demonstrate how to use a library resource or perform a complicated search? Jing let's you make short (five minutes or less) screen-capture videos at a moment's notice. You can also take and make notes on screenshots with Jing—there's no need for multiple or complicated tools. The software is produced by TechSmith, the same company that offers the paid tool Camstasia for longer video creation, and is available for Windows and Mac operating systems.

Jing allows you to create a screen-capture video and record audio voice-over of your entire screen or only a certain application. Videos are automatically uploaded to Screencast.com (they are hosted there for free), and users don't need any special software to view the videos, only an Internet connection. The only caveat is that you can't go back and edit your video or add written captions to video. However, for quick explanatory videos Jing can be the perfect tool.

After downloading, installing, and launching Jing, you will see a yellow sun on your desktop. This sun is used to control Jing and create videos at a moment's notice. Hover over the sun to see options for creating a capture, viewing videos you've already created, or adjusting the settings. Once you click the capture option, you can select part of your screen and immediately take a screenshot or start recording a video. When the recording is complete, the video will automatically upload to Screencast.com and you will be provided a link to the video that you can share with others. The videos are publicly available, and there is no registration or log-in required to watch a video. This makes access extremely easy but also means any sensitive information should not be shared using the tool.

Join.Me

While Jing is great for creating a screen capture or recording that is available for future viewing, Join.Me is specifically for in-the-moment screen sharing. It is great if you're on the phone or instant messaging someone and need to demonstrate some on-screen functionality. You can share your screen with up to ten people at a time using the free version of Join.Me, and there is no time limit to each session. Only the "hosts," the persons sharing their screen, need to install software on their computer; viewers of the meeting can join from their browser. The tool also provides a chat tool so participants can communicate within the interface and the ability to share screen control with viewers. Join.Me is built by the same company as LogMeIn, a software solution for remotely accessing your computer that is available for Windows and Mac operating systems.

To host a screen-sharing session, simply download, install, and launch the Join.Me software from the website. All you need to do is click the orange Start button to generate a meeting code and begin live sharing your screen. You will see a code appear at the top of the Join.Me window that looks like join.me/xxx-xxx-xxx. This is the address viewers will enter in their browser address bar in order to view your screen. If you click on the address, you can easily copy it to the clip-board and paste into an e-mail or instance message. You will know a viewer has joined your Join.Me session when a number appears next to the participant icon. To pause your screen sharing, you can click the largest button in the center of the Join.Me interface.

In addition to basic screen sharing, Join.Me offers some fantastic extras. You can set up a computer audio call by clicking the phone icon, allowing you to speak with participants through your computer. You can also use the chat icon to send instant messages to participants. When demonstrating something, it can be helpful to ask the viewers to try it themselves. This can be accomplished by clicking on a participant's name and giving him or her the ability to control your mouse. If you ever need to take back control, hit ESC on your keyboard. There's even the ability to present and view Join.Me meetings from your mobile device.

Google Hangouts

The primary use for Google Hangouts is video chat, but because of some of the great extras the tool offers, it can be used for effective online meetings or presentations as well. The advantage of using Google Hangouts is that you do not need to install any software onto your computer; everything is controlled through the browser. The only necessity is that you have a Google account. If your library and patrons already use Google Apps or Gmail, this tool can be a great solution. Many people already have a Google account through Gmail but don't realize it. The application also works via apps on mobile devices, so it can be accessed from anywhere.

You can have a meeting with up to ten people using Google Hangouts. In Gmail, make sure to turn on Google Hangouts, which replaces Google Chat and acts the same way. Think of Google Hangouts as Google Chat plus video chat, screen sharing, and other extras. To begin a video Google Hangout, simply start a chat with the person you want to invite from the Gmail screen. Then click the camera icon to start the video icon; this will automatically launch your webcam in the Google Hangout window. Use the person plus icon to add more people to the meeting.

MailChimp

Have you ever received a fantastically formatted e-mail from a company that included slick graphics with a complex layout and wondered, How'd they do that? Well, a lot of them are using MailChimp. MailChimp is a web application that provides an interface to create, send, and track e-mail newsletters. Using the free version of the product you can send up to twelve thousand e-mails to two thousand subscribers. There are also ways to view how many people open your e-mails and click on links that are included in them.

MailChimp has some specific lingo that can be helpful to understand before jumping in.

- List. The list of e-mail addresses of recipients of your e-mails. You can maintain multiple lists for different kinds of e-mails. You can manually add e-mails, upload a list from an Excel spreadsheet, or offer your patrons a web form where they can sign up for e-mails.
- Campaign. The e-mail message itself. When using MailChimp, one e-mail is the equivalent of a single campaign.
- Template. A saved design you can reuse for future e-mails. The template contains the colors, fonts, images, and layout that enhance the content of your e-mails. You can design templates when you create a new campaign or use a saved template.

To send an e-mail you'll need to first create a list of recipients. Even if you only have one recipient, or you want to send a test e-mail, you must create a list that contains at least one e-mail address. Once you have at least one list set up, you can create and send an e-mail using MailChimp.

When you click the Create Campaign button, you are offered four options. Use the Regular Ol' Campaign to create a basic e-mail. Follow the prompts (using the Next button at the bottom right of the screen) to select recipients; customize the e-mail options like Subject, From Address, Tracking, and Social Media; choose a template; design your e-mail; and send it.

The design stage of launching your e-mail is where you can get creative. Need some ideas? There is a great website, http://inspiration. mailchimp.com, where you can view examples of what others have made using MailChimp. MailChimp provides a drag-and-drop interface to set up your template, choose your colors, and enter your content. You can add other types of content to your template from the Content tab on the sidebar or change the colors and fonts from the Design tab. Once you are happy with the way your e-mail looks, you can move to the Confirm step and use the blue Send button to launch your campaign. After your campaign is launched, you can use the Reports to view how many people have opened your e-mail and clicked on links therein.

TOOLS FOR RESOURCE MANAGEMENT AND WEB DEVELOPMENT

WordPress

Perhaps you're familiar with WordPress as a blogging platform, but it's actually much more. You can certainly set up a blog, but the system is a great content-management platform that you can use to build a full-scale website. If you have a hand-coded website, you might wonder what is so great about using a content-management system (CMS), like WordPress, instead of maintaining a hand-coded website. A few reasons that using a CMS will make managing a website much easier are as follows:

- You can reuse content in multiple places; that way if you change your hours, for example, you only have to change them in one place.
- You can edit your website via the web, from anywhere, without special software. The editing tool automatically saves your content while you're working, so there's no accidental loss of edits.
- It is easy to select a theme (many are free) to have an attractive, responsive website without having any design or coding experience.
- You can control access to certain areas of the site, or the whole site, using the built-in security and user accounts functionality.
- WordPress.org allows you to make fancy website enhancements with a few clicks, such as social media integration, RSS feeds, image galleries, and e-mail subscriptions.

There are actually two flavors of WordPress that you should be familiar with before setting up a site: WordPress.com and WordPress.org.

- *WordPress.com* is a commercial website where you can set up your own website that is hosted by WordPress.com. You can set up a domain name for free, but it must include *.wordpress.com*. WordPress.com runs on the free software offered by WordPress.org. You can pay a small fee to remove the domain name and storage space restrictions. All backups and upgrades are done for you automatically through WordPress.com.

- *WordPress.org* is an open-source content-management system for managing websites and blogs. WordPress.org is software that you download and install on your own web server (that you manage yourself or pay a hosting company to manage for you). You are responsible for upgrading and backing up your site. Word-Press.org gives you the ability to customize any WordPress theme or build your own. You can also install plug-ins that allow you to do more with your site.

In this book we'll focus on using WordPress.com, because you can create a website for absolutely no cost. If you want to have total control over your site and ability to customize it, use WordPress.org instead. To set up WordPress.org, you'll need hosting space and a domain name, both of which can be purchased from a company such as A Small Orange (www.asmallorange.com) for less than one hundred dollars a year. This company, along with most hosting companies, offer a one-click install for WordPress, so you don't even need any programming or MySQL skills to get it up and running. If you want to install Word-Press.org manually (because you want to customize how the database or file structure is set up), you are able to do that as well.

Once you have your WordPress.com site up and running, you can begin creating the site content using the tools on the WordPress Dash-board. The WordPress Dashboard is where all the magic happens for your site. There are quite a few options in the WordPress Dashboard. Here are the most important for creating a basic website:

- Pages | *Create and edit the pages on your website.*
- Settings > General | *Manage basic settings like the site name and tagline.*
- Settings > Reading | *Front page settings and site visibility*
- Appearance > Themes | *Choose from various WordPress Themes. Use the Free link at the top right to only see free themes.*

WordPress.com is an easy way to try out using WordPress and build a test site. You can certainly use WordPress for building your entire public website, but there are other opportunities for libraries to use an online content-management platform, such as creating a staff intranet,

Figure 3.1. WordPress Dashboard, Pages

library blog, research guides, or knowledge base. If you're interested in learning more about WordPress, check out the book *WordPress for Libraries* by Chad Haefele, also in the Library Technology Essentials series.

AnyMeeting

AnyMeeting is a full-featured web-conferencing solution that is available, ad supported, for free. The functionality includes

- videoconferencing,
- screen sharing/control sharing,
- phone conferencing, and
- webinars.

With AnyMeeting you can use as little or as much of the functionality as you want. You can set up a webinar and invite people via e-mail or using a web link or you can only use the phone-conferencing option to coordinate an audio call. If you need a conference phone line, you can use www.freeconferencecall.com to obtain a free number. AnyMeeting is web based and runs inside a regular browser, so no downloads or installs are required for attendees; however, the host of the meeting needs to download a small desktop app to host the meeting. Using the free, ad-supported version, you can host meetings with up to two hundred people (up to six may use webcams).

AnyMeeting can be great to use in libraries in a variety of ways. Consider the possibility of hosting "virtual" programming or workshops where patrons can watch your presentations from their home computer or mobile device. This tool is also excellent for user instruction for distance or online patrons at an academic library.

Because there is so much robust functionality offered with AnyMeeting, it is best to hold a practice session before the live event. Be prepared to get the meeting set up early and expect to do some minor troubleshooting during the first five minutes of the meeting if people have questions about the tool. It is also a good idea to provide attendees with an overview of how AnyMeeting works and the best way for them to get in contact with you if they experience any issues during the meeting. Don't let the extra work deter you from using this tool, though. The functionality is equivalent to that of some very expensive paid tools and can vastly improve virtual communication once you are comfortable with it.

Google Calendar

You may have heard of or even used Google Calendar to keep track of personal appointments, but it has great potential for managing events, staffing, or the hours of operation for a library. Google Calendar provides an online calendar-management interface that can be kept private or made public. The calendar views are flexible and customizable; you can view a calendar by day, week, or month. They can be synced with personal devices and embedded on public websites.

To create and manage Google Calendars, you need to create an account with Google. You already have access to Google Calendar if you use Gmail or Google+. You can create events using the Create button on the upper, left corner of the calendar interface or by clicking on the specific date/time where you want to place an event on the calendar itself. You are also able to create multiple calendars and share individual calendars with other Google Calendars. For details on how to make a calendar public and embed a calendar on your website, check out the projects chapter (chapter 5).

There are many possibilities on how to use Google Calendar in libraries. Here are a few ideas to get you started. Use Google Calendar to manage the following:

- The display of library hours on your website (see featured example in chapter 4, the case studies chapter).
- Scheduling of staff at public service desks. For example, you can create an event for each shift and invite the staff member scheduled for that time to the event.
- Appointments that patrons make with library staff, such as research services appointments or time for scanning microfilm.
- Booking of rooms and display of room availability (see featured project in chapter 5, the projects chapter).

Google Forms

Google Forms is part of Google Drive, similar to Google Docs. With Google Forms you can build an online form that can be made public or shared via a link. Form answers are compiled in aggregate, so it is easy to view trends and, optionally, to view in a Google Sheet. When you create a form, you can select various question types such as multiple choice, checkboxes, free text, and scale. It is also possible to set up questions to direct users to another part of the form based on the answer the person selects. You may also set certain questions as required and download responses as a CSV. Google Forms can be a great tool for collecting data from library users and staff. Consider using Google Forms in the following ways:

- Collect basic statistics about questions asked at the reference desk.
- Create a satisfaction survey for patrons about library services or resources (see the example on collecting feedback in research guides in the case studies [chapter 4] for more details).
- Poll staff members about changes in library policy.
- Record student worker hours worked, via a "timesheet" form.

- Create a sign-up form for library events.

PosterOven and PosterMyWall

Unless you have a graphic design background, creating a visually appealing print-marketing campaign can be time consuming and difficult. Both PosterOven and PosterMyWall provide easy-to-use online interfaces for creating posters. You don't even need to create a user account in order to make a poster. There are a ton of premade, customizable templates to choose from, or you can create your own from scratch.

PosterOven focuses on creating posters that feature your organization's social media sites and the ability to automatically insert QR codes into the poster. Using the web-based "poster wizard," you can select a template, enter text and links, and print your finished poster in under ten minutes. Of course, you can always get more creative, change things around, or upload your own graphics. The final product is a downloadable pdf file you can print to your own printer, or have professionally printed.

PosterMyWall offers even more templates than PosterOven but is a bit more complex to use. If you don't have access to professional printing services, PosterMyWall also offers the ability to purchase physical poster copies through the site. If you had a look at PosterOven and thought, *I wish there were more options and custom graphics*, PosterMyWall is probably a better fit for your needs. There are a ton of background images, stock photos, and fancy fonts to choose from. However, more choice also means more time spent crafting your poster, so keep that in mind when deciding which tool to use.

Zoho Creator

Zoho Creator is an online relational database application. Imagine you combined the purpose of Microsoft Access with the online access offered by Google Docs. Zoho Creator allows you to build forms, reports, and web pages using a simple drag-and-drop interface. Even if you have no formal database experience, it's a cinch to set up a functional relational database in under an hour. If you do have some MySQL knowledge or programming skills, you can do lots of advanced reporting and scripting in Zoho Creator. So, why should you use a relational database?

What's the benefit of using a relational database instead of a spreadsheet? A 1988 article in *Business Computing* highlighted exactly why databases are better for large-scale data management (Brad Patten, "Database versus Spreadsheet Is No Contest," October 18, 1988, www.bizjournals.com). Their reasons include that databases are

- easier to share: more than one person can edit a database at the same time;
- more secure: private information is more secure, and it is harder for users to make a mistake;
- more efficient: duplication of data is reduced; and
- better for creating reports: it is easier to develop different views of a single set of data in a database.

There are many, many possibilities for using Zoho Creator in libraries. Any data that you want to be searchable and reportable is a great candidate for the tool. Here are a few ideas to get you started:

- Recording reference statistics or programs/instruction sessions
- Building a knowledge base/FAQ for service desks
- Managing library statistics for benchmark reports
- Keeping track of items on reserve for courses

Zoho Creator allows you to share up to three different applications with up to three people and have 250 records per user. If you want to create more applications, store more records, or publish your forms or reports (so they're accessible without a log-in), you'll need to obtain a license for the paid version, which is still relatively affordable with plans starting at sixty dollars a year. The setup and management of this application is done entirely through the web browser, so you don't need any additional hardware or services.

The following tools and applications require a bit more technical know-how to set up and manage. However, even a basic online course in one of the technologies they use is enough to learn the background skills you'll need. The technologies you'll need for success with CORAL and Guide on the Side are MySQL and PHP. A basic understanding of HTML, CSS, and JavaScript will be helpful with Sheetsee.js and HTML frameworks. For more information on recommended free online tutorials, see the "Helpful Technologies to Know" section of the introduction.

CORAL

CORAL is an open-source e-resources management (ERM) web application built by libraries, for libraries. It was originally developed by the Hesburgh Libraries at the University of Notre Dame. The application is made up of multiple modules that help you manage the workflow around e-resources. The main modules are as follows:

- Resources: document the metadata for each resource (database, e-journal, e-book package, etc.) your library subscribes to.
- Licensing: manage and track your digital copies of license agreements.
- Organizations: keep track of administrator accounts and contact information for e-resource vendors, publishers, and providers.
- Usage statistics: store and manage downloaded usage statistical reports from vendors.

CORAL can be customized to suit your library's needs. You can use as many or as few of the modules as you want to. Each module is made up of customizable forms where you can add and edit records and create relationships (between organizations and resources, for example). You are also able to search in the modules to quickly find the record you need to review or edit.

CORAL is a great alternative to expensive, proprietary ERM solutions and gives you more flexibility than a local spreadsheet or database. The application includes the ability to do the following:

- Create user accounts for staff members with different levels of permissions. For example, the e-resource librarian can be an administrator, with complete editing control, and a reference subject librarian could have viewing rights only.
- Access your e-resources metadata via the Internet, from any location.
- Build forms with customizable fields so you can include as much or as little detail as you need.

- Set up workflows for purchasing or renewing resources.

CORAL is built using a MySQL database, and the web interface is written in PHP. There is also some AJAX and jQuery that make the web interface work. However, you don't need to have programming experience to install CORAL. There is a web-installation process that works similar to installing a desktop application, but it is done through your browser. All you need to get CORAL up and running is a web server with MySQL and PHP. If you don't have your own web server, you can easily find web hosting online (more on this in the next chapter). To set up CORAL, follow these steps:

1. Download the files from https://github.com/ndlibersa/CORAL-Main by clicking the Download Zip button.
2. Upload the files to your web server using an FTP client such as FileZilla or Cyberduck. Note: An FTP client is used to transfer files from your computer to your web server. Refer to the "WordPress" section of this chapter to learn more about setting up your own inexpensive web server.
3. Navigate to the install folder for each module you want to set up. The path to the install folder looks like http://[yourservername]/coral/modulename/install/
4. Follow the directions in the web browser to set up the database, and finish the application setup.

If you're not ready to set up and install CORAL yet on your own web server, you can preview the software through a live demo on CORAL's website. Visit http://coraldemo.library.tamu.edu/usermanagement to request a user account. Once you've filled out the form, you can log in to the demo site, http://coraldemo.library.tamu.edu, using the username and password you've created.

CORAL has an active listserv and great step-by-step documentation for administrators and users on their website. If you're ready to try setting up CORAL on your own web server, check out the CORAL examples in chapters 4 and 5 for more details on implementation.

Guide on the Side

Guide on the Side (GotS) is a tutorial-building web application built by librarians at the University of Arizona for librarians. It provides library staff with an interface to build online, interactive tutorials "based on the principles of authentic and active learning" ("About Guide of the Side," University Libraries, accessed April 28, 2015, http://code.library. arizona.edu). Like the CORAL ERM solution, you can preview Guide on the Side by requesting a demo account at http://code.library.arizona. edu/contact. If you want to see tutorials created by other users, check out http://code.library.arizona.edu/gots-demo to get an idea of what you can build with GotS. See figure 3.2 for an example screenshot.

Using Guide on the Side you can build tutorials that sit inside the browser window and walk the user through using your website, discovery interface, online catalog, or any other part of your library's online presence. Guide creators can build content by using the online WYSIWYG (what you see is what you get) interface—no coding experience is necessary. It is easy to set up a linked table of contents, add and format text, create headings, and insert pictures and questions. There are also the options to have a graded quiz or a form where users can

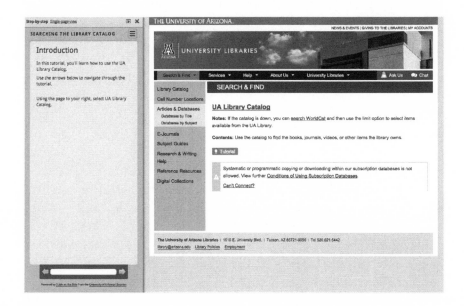

Figure 3.2. Guide on the Side

submit feedback at the end of the tutorial. Users can also view all the instructions in a single list, if they prefer that to the step-by-step integrated tutorial. It is up to the user to advance the tutorial and answer the questions; the guide itself isn't able to "see" what the user is actually clicking on within the website.

Details on setting up GotS are available in the README file on GitHub, along with the software download. You will need a web server with PHP and MySQL in order to host the web application. For this application it is helpful to have a bit of background knowledge on MySQL in order to set up the database and install the application. Even if you have only a cursory knowledge, you should be able to get the application up and running by following the instructions. There is a Google Group where you can ask questions of the application creators and other users who are available for further help: "Guide on the Side Discussion," Google Groups, accessed April 29, 2015, https://groups. google.com.

Sheetsee.js

Sheetsee.js is a code library that allows you to build impressive data visualizations on your website from data stored in a simple Google Sheet. Using this code library *does* require a bit of background knowledge of HTML, CSS, and JavaScript, but it is a great web-development project for a beginner looking to learn more and create something fantastic without having to code from scratch. You'll need to have access to your website's source code where you want to put Sheetsee.js in order to use it. The original code was created for cities and towns as a way to publish budget numbers on their websites. However, there are great opportunities for libraries to use this code as well to publish statistics, share budget numbers, or showcase collections data.

There are three types of visualizations Sheetsee.js can create for you: tables, charts, and maps. You can download the code from GitHub (Jessica Lord [jlord], "Sheetsee-Core," accessed April 29, 2015, https:// github.com). You'll also need to create a Google Sheet that will feed Sheetsee.js. It is important that all of the columns in your spreadsheet have easy-to-understand headings and do not have any merged cells, because it will make it easier for Sheetsee.js to understand your data.

To get started with Sheetsee.js after downloading the source code from GitHub, follow the basic instructions at Jessica Lord (jlord), "Spreadsheets as Databases," accessed April 29, 2015, http://jlord.us. Read through the directions first; then begin editing the code in the files you've downloaded. It may seem slightly overwhelming, but remember, you're just following directions and replacing some text, not coding a whole solution from scratch. For a more in-depth examination of visualizing data, check out the book *Data Visualizations and Infographics*, by Sarah Maudlin, also in the Library Technology Essentials series.

HTML Frameworks and Templates

There is a great selection of premade, fully functional and responsive HTML website frameworks and templates for you to download online—*if* you know where to look. These tools are basically full-scale websites that are already built for you using HTML, CSS, and JavaScript. All you have to do is customize the content, such as the text, links, and images, to match your needs. If you have some experience editing web files, but don't have the time or skills to design something from scratch, using a framework or template is a fantastic way to create something professional looking with minimal effort. So what exactly are these frameworks and templates? Let's look at each category and a few examples you can download and get started with right now.

An HTML framework is a package of standardized code files, usually HTML, CSS, and JavaScript, that can be the basis for building a website. Since most websites have a similar structure, there's no need for you to reinvent the wheel by building one entirely from scratch! Frameworks are what the professionals use to make their web design and development lives much easier. Many of these frameworks are built on a grid system and are automatically responsive if a user is accessing from a mobile device.

If you've used LibGuides 2.0, then you've used a site built on the Bootstrap framework (http://getbootstrap.com), which is a freely available open-source framework, originally built by Twitter. You can download all of the files that make a nice responsive website from the Get Bootstrap site. A few other frameworks you might consider include the following:

- Foundation (http://foundation.zurb.com): Offers lots of fancy interface gadgets with thorough documentation. Uses CSS and JavaScript libraries.
- Skeleton (www.getskeleton.com): A good basic framework. Uses CSS only.

Depending on your needs, you might chose one framework over another. Although Foundation offers lots of cool interface enhancements, Skeleton is much simpler to get up and running. To see a comparison of Bootstrap, Foundation, and Skeleton, visit "Responsive CSS Framework Comparison," Vermilion Design, last updated December 22, 2014, http://responsive.vermilion.com.

If you don't have the bandwidth to dive into an HTML framework, finding a template can be an even better opportunity. With a template you're basically downloading a website that is already built and designed for you. The only thing you have to do is alter the content and upload the files to your web server. There are a myriad of free templates available from many websites, but I recommend checking out W3 Layouts (http://w3layouts.com) because their site features only free templates, and they are easy to download and customize with your own content. They do require that you put a back link to their site in your website's footer. If you want to remove the back link, there is a onetime cost of ten dollars.

There are hundreds of templates to pick from on this site, and you can choose any one you'd like. There is even a responsive library template! (See "Public Library Education Mobile Website Template," W3 Layouts, November 5, 2013, http://w3layouts.com.) Once you download the files you will need to customize the content for your organization. To read more about using this HTML template check out chapter 5.

Public Library Education Mobile Website Template

Figure 3.3. Responsive website template

4

LIBRARY EXAMPLES AND CASE STUDIES

Now that you have a handle on the background of some library technology tools, let's examine some organizations that are using these tools in innovative and inspiring ways. One of the best ways to get ideas and gain confidence in your ability to implement these solutions is to hear about how others have been successful. It's also helpful to understand how to avoid any issues that others encountered and what future plans they have for the tool. These case studies cover a variety of libraries, but the approaches taken can be adapted to any organization.

USING GOOGLE FORMS FOR LIBGUIDES FEEDBACK

Middlebury College | Stacy Reardon, Research and Instruction Librarian

Stacy Reardon is a research and instruction librarian at Middlebury College in Vermont. Middlebury College is a residential liberal arts college. The college serves about 2,450 undergraduate students and has a nine-to-one student-faculty ratio ("Quick Facts," Middlebury, accessed April 29, 2015, www.middlebury.edu). Stacy oversees reference services and outreach for foreign language, anthropology, and gender studies students. A portion of her job is to manage the research guides on the LibGuides platform for these areas of study and make them as easy to use as possible. Stacy includes a Google Form on each guide she manages where users can provide her with direct feedback about the guide.

The idea of including a feedback form on a LibGuide seems simple enough; LibGuides even offers a stock "feedback" box type. However, Stacy wanted to have more flexibility around the presentation of the form and the type of data she collected. Instead of using the LibGuides feedback box, she utilized Google Forms to build a very simple form for collecting feedback and took advantage of the built-in notifications feature. Stacy's approach makes the user experience as simple as possible and eliminates the need for her to check the submissions regularly through use of the automatic alert e-mails.

Stacy's main goal was to make it as easy as possible for the user to complete the form; she only includes a single field: Suggestions for this Guide. Since Stacy maintains multiple guides, she had to create an individual Google Form for each guide, so she would know from where the submission originates. She could have used a single form and added another question that asked users to select which guide they were on from a drop-down menu, but that wouldn't be as easy for the user to complete. The first step Stacy took was to create a Google Form for each guide and to make sure the name of the form coincided with the guide where she would embed it. Each form contained one "essay"-style question, Suggestions for this Guide, and allowed the users to edit their responses if desired.

After creating a form for each guide she managed, Stacy set up the notifications so she would receive an e-mail when the form was submitted. This is convenient because she doesn't need to periodically check the form in Google Docs to see if anyone has submitted feedback. If you want to use this functionality, you'll need to create a Google Sheet and then create a form that will populate the sheet. To enable notifications on a Google Form, follow these steps:

1. Create a new Google Sheet.
2. In your Google Sheet, select the Tools menu and select Create a Form.
3. Add the question to your form, and save your form. Return to the Google Sheet.
4. From the Google Sheet, select the Tools menu, and select Notification Rules. The Notification Rules window will appear.

5. Select Notify Me . . . When a User Submits a Form, and choose whether you want to receive e-mails immediately or as a daily digest.

Your form notifications are now ready to go.

Once Stacy created the forms and setup notifications, she added them to each of her guides. At Middlebury College they have included the feedback forms on the guide's landing page at the bottom, so it doesn't take precedence over the main content but is still a presence on the most-visited page of each guide. In order to embed the form on the guide, create an HTML content box in LibGuides and retrieve the embed code for your form. Follow these steps to get the embed code in Google Forms:

1. Navigate to your Google Form.
2. Select the File menu item and click Embed . . .
3. Determine appropriate width and height. Your form should be based on the width and height of your HTML content box in LibGuides to make the form display properly.
4. Enter the dimensions in the Custom Size height and width fields.
5. Copy the HTML text beginning with <iframe> from the Embed Form window.
6. In LibGuides, edit your HTML content box, and paste in the <iframe> code you copied from Google Forms. Your form will now display in your guide.

Using a simple Google Form on your research guides, or on any website, is a fantastic way to collect feedback from users. Stacy's user-focused approach might be a bit more work for the initial setup but makes it as easy as possible for someone to complete the form. Although your institution's content-management systems may offer built-in feedback forms, using a Google Form can provide more flexibility in the kind of questions you can ask users. With Google Forms you'll also have the ability to collect qualitative or quantitative data depending on the types of questions you ask.

It is often a good idea to consider using a free tool to enhance an existing system; don't assume that a paid or existing solution is always the best for the user. Although it is a bit more work during setup to make individual forms for each guide/page, this approach ensures a better user experience, and it is more likely that you'll receive user feedback if the submission process is as easy as possible. Stacy's approach to collecting feedback on her LibGuides continues to be a success because she had a clear goal to make the experience as easy as possible for the user.

BUILDING A LEARNING COMMONS INTRANET WITH WORDPRESS

Daytona State College | Cheryl Kohen, Emerging Technology Librarian

Cheryl Kohen is the emerging technology librarian at Daytona State College (DSC) in eastern Florida. DSC is a public college with over one hundred certificate, associate's, and bachelor's degree programs. The college enrolls about twenty-eight thousand students each year and offers eleven bachelor's degree programs ("About Daytona State," Daytona State College, last updated March 31, 2015, www.daytonastate.edu). Cheryl's role at the DSC Library is to oversee new technology initiatives and advocate for innovative technology adoption.

When Cheryl began her new role at DSC, she observed the staff of the Learning Commons was heavily dependent on e-mail for internal communications. There is nothing fundamentally wrong with this approach, but there are free tools available to improve these types of communication between the staff. Part of Cheryl's job is to introduce new technologies to the library that improve efficiency and streamline workflows. She knew there was a solution for organizing and archiving messaging between the staff, similar to an approach she had used at a previous job. She suggested creating a WordPress blog for sharing announcements, news, and policy updates to reduce the number of e-mails that were exchanged between staff for these purposes.

The creation of the WordPress site was based on a specific need Cheryl identified. As part of the planning process, Cheryl also crafted goals for the site. The main goals of the WordPress site were to

- reduce e-mail updates about news, events, and announcements;
- establish a searchable archive for this type of content; and

- create a foundational site for new employees where they can learn about recent Learning Commons news.

Cheryl led the initiative to roll out the WordPress site and made sure to clearly articulate its purpose and audience. She determined the audience for the site would include staff from the following departments:

- library
- Academic Support Center
- Writing Center
- Technology Help Desk
- Faculty Innovation Center

Including these groups of staff made it even easier to keep the lines of communication open and facilitate collaboration. The decision was also made to keep the site internal to staff members only, since the information discussed was not intended for the student and faculty populations.

Cheryl also outlined the specific functionality of the WordPress site. She created a succinct proposal to explain the purpose of the site and included the following functionalities as key points to explain the purpose of the site to stakeholders and future users:

- Users may post news updates, happenings, and activities that affect members of the Learning Commons.
- Users may upload documents, images, and shared files.
- Users may subscribe and receive posts and comments via e-mail as an alert for new content. All members of the Learning Commons may register using WordPress and log on at least once to receive these notifications.
- Posts are searchable by users, creating a repository of information that can be accessed by members of the Learning Commons.
- All content posted within the blog will be password protected and will not be searchable by nonmembers of the Learning Commons.
- Links to the directories of each department will be available within the Learning Commons.

There was minimal technical skill required to create and set up a free WordPress site using WordPress.com. The parts of the WordPress site include the following:

- Blog Posts—This content is on the home page.
- About—Describes the purpose and audience of the site.
- FAQs for Service Points—A quick list of common questions asked at library service desks.
- Links to library handouts and room-booking calendars.

Once the site was set up, users from each audience were informed of the new site and invited to create accounts in order to access and contribute content. Cheryl also recommended that users subscribe to new posts on the blog via e-mail, to receive an automatic notification when new content is posted. Adoption of the site has been strong, and the site has accomplished the goals of reducing e-mail announcements and establishing a searchable archive of news. New employees have used the site successfully to learn about the culture of the Learning Commons.

Cheryl identified one future goal of purchasing a specific domain name for the WordPress site. Currently, the site uses a free domain name that includes .wordpress.com as part of the URL. A proprietary domain name would be easier to remember and make the URL much cleaner. When the site was originally launched, there was no budget for the domain name, but that didn't impede the site from being successful.

There are many ways to use a free content-management system, like WordPress, in a library environment. Cheryl's project to implement WordPress as an intranet for the staff of the Learning Commons at DSC was successful because the technology was used to address an identified need. Thoughtful planning ensured adoption and contributions would be consistent among the staff members using the platform. By focusing on what she was able to do with the resources available, she was able to accomplish the main project goals without using any budget funds. Cheryl's approach makes great use of this free technology tool and has vastly improved the communication workflow at her library. If you'd like to set up something similar in your library, check out the first project in chapter 5 of this book.

CREATING A NEW MATERIALS NEWSLETTER USING MAILCHIMP

Harris-Elmore Public Library | Jennifer Fording, Local History Librarian

The Harris-Elmore Public Library is located about twenty miles south of Toledo, Ohio, and has a staff of seven people, including two pages. The library wanted an easy way to promote readers' advisory and decided to try distributing lists of new young adult materials to interested patrons. Before using MailChimp for new materials newsletters, the only way patrons at the Harris-Elmore Public Library could see a list of new items was to come into the library and view a paper printout. Jennifer Fording, the library's local history librarian, wanted to make it easier to promote readers' advisory for patrons and saw a great opportunity to use MailChimp to accomplish this goal.

Like many libraries, Harris-Elmore Public did not have the funds to buy a proprietary readers' advisory tool but wanted to promote their new acquisitions to their community. The library piloted creating and sending MailChimp newsletters with their young adult materials and eventually used it to promote new additions to all of their collections. Knowing that a paid solution would not be feasible for her library, Jennifer researched easy ways to build professional-looking e-mail newsletters online. She discovered MailChimp and was able to quickly create an e-mail template that could be updated each month with new materials. Jennifer describes MailChimp as "streamlined and very easy to set up."

Jennifer also set up an online form that she embedded into her library's website where patrons could sign up for these e-mail newsletters of new materials. Finally, she promoted the e-mail newsletter to her community. The promotions for the new materials newsletters included the following:

- Announcements at in-person events
- Advertising in the local newspaper
- Advertisements on library signage

- Social media announcements (MailChimp has a built-in function where you can link to the newsletter as a web page if people want to view without signing up)
- Bookmarks in the library

Once the young adult e-mail newsletter was set up, it became popular and Jennifer decided to create similar newsletters for other areas of the collection and related forms where patrons could subscribe. Currently, the library offers the following new materials e-mail lists:

- Adult fiction
- Adult nonfiction
- Young adult fiction
- Juvenile fiction
- Juvenile nonfiction
- Easy/beginner reader
- Audiobooks
- Large-print books
- DVDs
- CDs
- Cookbooks

Managing the updates to these newsletters has become part of Jennifer's job, but often the updates are delegated to library pages. In order to update the newsletters every month, the library staff member will collect information from the appropriate purchase orders, get cover art and a book synopsis from Amazon, and update the MailChimp template. The newsletters also include a sidebar where library events are promoted.

The statistics that MailChimp provides have proved helpful for developing and tweaking the e-mail campaigns. The basic statistics in MailChimp indicate how many people are subscribed to the campaign and how many people actually open the e-mail. One tweak Jennifer made after the first few e-mails was to shorten the list of items, because including all the materials was somewhat overwhelming. Now, instead of listing every new item, the newsletters include the books that are the most popular and specific items the library wants to promote.

The MailChimp newsletters have been very successful for Harris-Elmore Public Library. After a few months of introducing the e-mail newsletter, there are over 150 people signed up. When Jennifer originally saw other public libraries doing something similar with a paid solution, she was inspired to find a similar solution that was affordable for her library. Using MailChimp was simple to implement and easy to maintain. In addition to new materials, the library is able to publicize events and other notices via the e-mail campaigns. In the future they intend to keep up the MailChimp newsletters for new materials promotion because it is a simple and free way to promote resources and services to patrons.

IMPLEMENTING CORAL FOR E-RESOURCES MANAGEMENT

Fenway Libraries Online | Kelly Drake, Systems Librarian

Fenway Libraries Online, or FLO, is a consortium of academic and special libraries located in and around Boston. Member institutions share resources and systems, as well as decision making, on all aspects of library automation (http://flo.org). The FLO systems librarian, Kelly Drake, is part of the FLO team that oversees all systems, including the integrated library system (ILS), link resolver, and proxy server for the organization.

After receiving feedback from a consortium member survey that e-resources workflow needed improvement and streamlining, Kelly led an investigation into deploying a unified e-resources management system. A majority of the libraries were unhappy with their systems and were dissatisfied with the lack of organization between institutions. The result of the investigation into e-resources management systems led to the implementation of the open-source platform CORAL.

Kelly wanted to understand what the specific problems and requirements were among the consortium libraries before considering solutions. Through a second survey, focused on e-resources management, Kelly determined the main issues were as follows:

- There were too many places where staff needed to enter data about e-resources.

- Record keeping could be more organized, and the process differed from institution to institution.
- There was an unnecessary duplication of shared resource details like consortial subscriptions and state-provided databases.

Marilyn Geller, the collection management librarian from Lesley University, shared details about what her library used to manage e-resources before adopting CORAL: "For several years, we were using a homegrown Access database. It was not a polished product, and it was only available to one person on one computer. It had serious limitations and flaws. . . . Because the homegrown database had so many problems, it never fully became part of the digital resources management landscape within the library." Based on the identified problems, such as those Marilyn described, Kelly determined the main requirements were that the system reduce data duplication and be easy to maintain, so that users would see the system as an asset instead of a hindrance in managing the e-resources lifecycle.

Since FLO shares all decision making, a small committee was formed to determine the best platform for e-resources management. Kelly put together a team of eight library staff members including representatives from institutions that were experiencing the most issues around e-resources management. An intern performed an external scan of what systems were available and an internal scan of what systems could be easily supported by FLO.

The project team examined three systems in depth and piloted two: CORAL and a paid solution. Kelly says CORAL was selected because "it just makes sense." She explains that even staff members who aren't managing e-resources understand the workflow based on how the system is organized. It was also cost effective; since FLO already had the local server infrastructure to host CORAL, there was no monetary cost to implement the system. The CORAL community support and excellent documentation also helped convince the team it was the best solution for their needs.

Once the decision was made to select CORAL as the e-resources management solution for FLO, the software was downloaded from the CORAL website and installed on FLO's existing web server. CORAL consists of multiple modules: Resources, Licensing, Organizations, and Usage Statistics. Not all modules are required for the system, but FLO decided to set up each of them and focus on populating the Organizations and Resources modules first. Librarian Marilyn Geller said that they "found that adding all of the Organizations first, and then adding Resources, seems to be the most logical way to fill up the database. After that, you can progress to the licensing module." The Organizations module contains information about vendors, whereas the entries in the Resources module represent e-resource products that are provided by specific organizations.

Because there are ten different institutions sharing a single system, the team wanted to make sure there was consistency in how entries were made. The project group created a simple data dictionary that system users refer to as a guide when entering their information into CORAL. This ensures there aren't any discrepancies in how entries are named. The glossary is available online via the CORAL software repository, hosted on GitHub, for others to use (Louisa A. Choy, "CORAL—Main: Glossary of Terms and Fields," GitHub, last updated September 20, 2013, https://github.com).

The data entry was divided into two phases:

1. Members of the original system-selection team entered their data and created training materials based on their experience.
2. The project team held hands-on training sessions with staff from other institutions to finish entering all electronic resources used by members of FLO into CORAL.

The implementation of CORAL for the FLO libraries, including setting up the system and entering the bulk of the data, took about one year from start to finish. Marilyn and Kelly both noted that for single libraries the setup and data population would be much quicker because there doesn't need to be the level of coordination and collaboration between multiple institutions.

The group was able to accomplish its goals of minimizing repetitive data entry, organizing e-resource records, and reducing duplication of data across disparate systems. However, the work on the system continues at a high rate. Member institutions use the system regularly to add and update records as needed. Some institutions have begun using the Terms tool add-on, which allows staff members to view key parts of license agreements stored in CORAL, without actually having access to the CORAL licensing module. The project team also plans to contribute to the CORAL code base by building a cost-history enhancement to the Resources module. The system is easy for library staff to maintain and is flexible enough to adapt to any additional metadata they might want to track in the future. Overall, the consortium is very happy with CORAL and has seen a tremendous improvement in managing e-resources workflow since the implementation.

GUIDE ON THE SIDE FOR FEATURED RESOURCE TUTORIALS

Pima County Public Library | Jenny Gubernick, Web Development Librarian

Pima County Public Library is located in and around Tucson, Arizona. It is made up of twenty-seven libraries and employs over five hundred people. There are around 442,000 cardholders. Below is an interview with Jenny Gubernick, who is responsible for technology training for a range of topics, both internal and patron facing, as well as managing the website at the Pima County Public Library. Jenny uses the open-source tool Guide on the Side for building online tutorials for electronic resources.

Question: How Do You Use Guide on the Side?

Answer:

We do a featured resource every two months or so—there's a big marketing push, staff training in person, and then we make a Guide on the Side available for staff first, and then also to the public after staff has become familiar with it.

We don't do a guide for every featured resource, though, and sometimes we do guides just for something we've had a lot of questions about from the public. For example, we have created a tutorial for using NoveList, a reader's advisory database, and for using Freading, which is an online e-book service. We try to make guides for resources that are popular yet have somewhat counterintuitive or confusing websites.

Question: Did You Consider Using a Different Tool for a Similar Purpose? What Were You Using before This Tool?

Answer:

Yes, and we still do kind of take a several-pronged approach depending on the resource. We've done short videos using Camtasia and Jing, handouts with screenshots, in-person workshops for both staff and public. This has just given us another option.

Question: How Much Time Does It Take to Create and Maintain Tutorials? Do You Have Any Help from Others on the Staff?

Answer:

I'll use Freading as an example—that took me about five hours to create the initial content, take screenshots, and learn how to use the website enough to guide people through it! (If it hadn't been a new product, it probably would have been faster.) Then I sent it out to increasingly large groups of staff for feedback and revised it based on their feedback. That only took a few minutes at a time but probably added up to another hour of work that's ongoing as we hear from people. Also, about two months in, Freading redesigned their website and I had to spend a few minutes taking new screenshots and rewriting some of the text— that was about fifteen or twenty minutes, if I recall correctly.

Another example: for NoveList, it took two people about two hours to write the chapter headings and content (we split that up). Then it took the rest of the team a few more hours to add screenshots, expand the content, add Q&A, et cetera. It probably took the same number of hours total when it was the whole team collaborating.

Question: What Are Your Tips for Others Interested in Using This Tool?

Answer:

The number one thing you need is good writers! This has been a little tough at PCPL—we've had really excellent work on the team, and then those people tend to get new jobs or assigned to different duties, and new people have to start over in relearning the tone and content. We try to incorporate humor and use a tone that's friendly and conversational, like we would explain to a customer in person. The UA Library has some best practices on their website as far as using paragraphs, bullet points, breaking it up into small pieces, et cetera, that is very helpful.

Question: Do You Have Future Plans for Expanding or Enhancing Your Usage of Guide on the Side?

Answer:

It really depends on the number of people on our team, and also on our IT setup—if we ever get a server where we can host it, there are a lot of resources with weird restrictions that we might be able to make guides for. However, the biggest limitation is just staff time and finding staff with the skills and interest. Plus, ideally our website and resources will be intuitive enough that we don't need to train our staff and customers how to use them! Unlike with academic libraries, we focus on giving a friendly intro for someone's first visit to a resource, rather than tips for power users.

You can view the tutorial from the Pima County Public Library on the resource Freading, at "Freading Quick Start," accessed April 29, 2015, http://pcpl-tutorials.library.arizona.edu.

MANAGING LIBRARY HOURS WEBSITE DISPLAY WITH GOOGLE CALENDAR

Assumption College | Mary Brunelle, Head of Library Systems and Technology

Assumption College is a private, primarily undergraduate Catholic college located in Worcester, Massachusetts. It has about two thousand undergraduate students and a twelve-to-one student-faculty ratio. Mary Brunelle is the sole library staff member who is devoted to supporting library systems and technology at the Emmanuel d'Alzon Library. When the library migrated to using Drupal to manage their website, she was interested in finding a better solution for displaying the library's hours of operation on the website. Previously, library staff used a home-grown HTML script developed by the information technology (IT) department that had to be updated weekly. Now, she has moved to using

Google Calendar to provide an easy-to-read view of library hours and events.

Mary wanted to present a comprehensive view of library hours and events on the website, and also wanted to use a system that was easy to update. This way other staff, such as the access services librarian, could update the hours page on the website, without actually having to make direct edits in Drupal. The college's webmaster suggested using Google Calendar because it is familiar to many people and it is easy to maintain multiple repeating events.

Once the tool was selected, Mary had to iron out the implementation details. There are two Google Calendars displayed in a single calendar view on the library's hours page. The first calendar is for the hours open, and the other is used for special events. She decided to use repeating events in Google Calendar to display the hours open, since the library doesn't have many exceptions to its schedule throughout the semester. This approach significantly cut down the number of entries she needed to make in the calendar to maintain the hours. On holidays there is a separate entry with the name of the holiday so it is easy to see.

The events calendar is an entire separate calendar in Google but is displayed together with the hours-open calendar on the library website. This is helpful because the person who maintains the events calendar might not be different than the person tasked with updating the hours-open calendar. This way staff members only have rights to access what they need, but the public only sees a single cohesive calendar. See figure 4.1 for an example of what the final calendar looks like displayed in the website. Hours are displayed in dark blue, events in green, and holidays in purple.

After setting up the hours of operation and special events, the calendar was ready to be embedded in the hours page on the library's website.

The Google Calendar is embedded into the Drupal page using an iframe. An iframe, short for inline frame, is an HTML tag that allows you to embed an external web page in your web page. There is built-in functionality in Google Calendar to create an iframe using any type of calendar view. To embed a Google Calendar in your website using an iframe, follow the instructions from the "Managing Meeting Space with Google Calendar" project in chapter 5.

Figure 4.1.   Emmanuel d'Alzon Library hours calendar embedded

Using Google Calendar for the hours page at the Emmanuel d'Alzon Library at Assumption College has been a successful, simple way for the staff to manage library hours and events. This approach allows staff members to update the hours page even if they don't have editor privileges in Drupal. The only thing they need is access to the Google Calendar. Implementing Google Calendar has not only improved the look of the library hours page but also significantly decreased the amount of time library staff need to maintain it.

USING JING AND SCREENMARKER FOR PROFESSIONAL-LOOKING VIDEO TUTORIALS

Seminole State College of Florida | Nichole Martin, Instructional Technology Librarian

Seminole State College of Florida is a public, undergraduate college with four campuses located in central Florida. There are about twenty thousand students enrolled and over 780 faculty members ("Seminole State College of Florida: Fast Facts," August 2011, www.seminolestate. edu). Nichole Martin wears many hats as the instructional technology librarian, including providing research services for online students, managing library web resources, such as YouTube and LibGuides, along with creating video tutorials for staff and patrons. Nichole devised a way to use two free tools in conjunction to make professional and polished video tutorials that she primarily uses for online students.

Previously, Nichole had used Captivate to create video tutorials, but she wanted something that was easier to use to create videos "on the fly" that didn't require a lot of editing or enhancements. She did some Internet research and decided to use Jing for creating quick tutorials. She says Jing is great because "it replicates the one-on-one type interaction I'd be able to have at the reference desk" for online patron requests. Jing launches quickly via the desktop widget and has become part of her "librarian tool belt," as she puts it. Because it automatically uploads a video to Screencast.com when you're done, there's virtually no wait time for rendering the video or uploading it to a host site like YouTube.

Pairing Jing with the free tool ScreenMarker gives the creator more options and makes video tutorials even more professional looking. Jing gives you the ability to record and publish your videos, but there isn't an easy way to visually call out parts of the screen while recording. Screen-Marker gives you a marker tool to circle, highlight, and draw on your screen in real time. You can use it during any kind of presentation, or while recording your screen with Jing to call attention to certain parts of the screen. Nichole uses the two tools together to make her tutorials easy to follow.

Jing and ScreenMarker are great to use together for demonstrating how to use library resources to do research. Nichole is an embedded librarian for an online English course and had a student struggling to find articles for a research paper that met the instructor's requirements. Nichole created several short videos, one for each database, to demonstrate search strategies and filter by certain criteria. If she had to write the steps out or explain them over the phone, it would have been a cumbersome process. Using Jing and ScreenMarker made it much easier to show how to do the searching, rather than only telling.

Although Jing is great for quick tutorials, it does have some limitations. Nichole notes that it can be difficult to stick to the five-minute time limit and inability to edit recordings, but it is easy to rerecord a video since they are so short. Nichole also shared some excellent tips for users who are new to creating video tutorials with Jing:

- If there is a lengthy loading time for a web page, click the pause button to save time and make the video as quick as possible.
- Consider screen size when recording. You may have a large monitor, but most people do not. She recommends resizing the browser to be slightly smaller than full screen. Screencast.com won't resize your content for you as do YouTube or Vimeo. Always preview the video in Screencast.com to get an idea of what the user will see.
- Make sure to capture the whole browser in the Jing window—don't leave off the scroll bar. It can be disorienting not to see the mouse moving around. This way the viewer can see exactly what you're doing. You need to really consider the user's view in all aspects of video tutorial creation.

Combining Jing and ScreenMarker is a great way to produce professional-looking video tutorials. Nichole has used this approach successfully with online students as a way to demonstrate different aspects of the research process, but it could be adapted for a variety of uses.

5

STEP-BY-STEP PROJECTS FOR FREE TECHNOLOGY

Now that we've covered the details about a myriad of free technology tools, let's take a look at some real-world library projects. These projects detail how to use a free software or service to tackle common library issues. The purpose of using these technologies is to improve your library's organization and management. Each project can be easily adapted for whatever circumstances exist in your own organization.

HOW TO MANAGE INTERNAL POLICY AND PROCEDURE DOCUMENTATION USING WORDPRESS

Most libraries keep documentation about policies and procedures on patron services in a handbook or physical format. Your library might have a printed copy of this documentation at service desks or as a Microsoft Word document on a shared drive. There is nothing wrong with keeping physical documentation, but with many services being conducted virtually, there are many benefits to making your documentation available to staff on the web.

Migrating to an online system, like WordPress, for hosting internal documentation makes maintaining and accessing information much easier for staff. Although WordPress is widely known as a blogging platform, it can also act as a content-management system or CMS. A content-management system is an easy way to create a website without having to do any hand coding. You can create pages to hold the content of a staff handbook, and assigning parent pages creates the site's organizational structure. And instead of blog posts, you can announce updates and news related to the service desks. The benefits of moving internal documentation online to WordPress include the following:

- the documentation is accessible from any computer with an Internet connection, and pages can still be printed via WordPress if it is important for a physical copy of the handbook to exist;
- WordPress provides a space for multiple authors to facilitate content collaboration;
- individual user accounts can be created for content owners and readers;
- WordPress provides built-in, comprehensive search functionality; and
- it is eco-friendly (as you'll no longer be regularly printing a physical policy manual).

The only investment is staff time to complete the initial platform setup and content migration.

Setting Up Your WordPress Site

The WordPress setup portion of the project can happen in tandem with the content organization efforts or after the content is prepped and ready to be entered in the site. In order to set up WordPress, the first decision to make is whether to use WordPress.org or WordPress.com.

There is a more in-depth overview of WordPress.com versus WordPress.org on the WordPress support site ("Support: WordPress.com and WordPress.org," WordPress.com, accessed April 29, 2015, http://en.support.wordpress.com). You can also check out *WordPress for Libraries* by Chad Haefele from this same series for more great details about WordPress.

- *WordPress.org*. You host the website yourself. You'll need web space where you host your own website. There is usually a cost associated with the web space, but your library might have available web space if you are hosting your own website already. The benefits of using WordPress.org are that you can customize your theme, install plug-ins, and have more control over your site.

- *WordPress.com.* WordPress will host your site for you. All you need to maintain is the content. You will need to use a site name such as [yoursitename].wordpress.com, unless you purchase your own domain name. A domain name, such as www.amazon.com, can be purchased through any web-hosting company. There is an interface in the WordPress Dashboard for connecting a purchased domain name to your site.

For this example, we will use the WordPress.com solution.

In addition to selecting the type of WordPress site, you'll need to make several decisions about how the site will be set up.

- *Will content be publicly accessible or private and password protected?* If you choose to password protect the content, you will need to create accounts for each user. Even for a public site you will need to create user accounts for the content owners so they can enter and maintain content.
- *What will your site look like?* Many theme options are available for WordPress.com. Since the bulk of the content is text based, select a basic theme that is made for written content and is easy to navigate. Stay away from themes that are intended for showcasing visual items such as videos or photos, since the majority of your content will most likely be text based.
- *What will your site be named?* You will need to enter a web address for your site during the WordPress setup.
- *Which e-mail address will the WordPress account be associated with?* Use an institutional e-mail address, such as library@myschool.org, instead of a person's e-mail address.

For the example project we will assume the following:

- The site will be restricted to staff use only and not available to the public. Each staff member will need an account.
- The site will use the Twenty Twelve theme available for free through WordPress.
- The site will be named librarystaffhandbook.wordpress.com.

- The e-mail address used to set up the site will be library@mytown.org.

The staff person deemed the WordPress administrator will follow the setup instructions on WordPress.com to create the site. Once the site is created, the site structure and permissions will be set up using the following steps:

Organizing Your Content

Before any system setup is done in WordPress, have discussions with other staff members about content. The content owners need to determine the best way to organize the content on the WordPress site. Consider how staff members actually use the information. Speak with staff members who work at the service desks in order to determine the best way to organize this information on the new site.

The existing handbook is organized in two sections, "Policies" and "Procedures." Speak with your staff to determine the best organizational structure for your library. Here's one example: you may choose to organize your content into four segments based on the four functional areas of the organization: General Library, Reference, Circulation, and Technology. The General Library information will appear on the main page of the site. Reference, Circulation, and Technology will be the top-level navigational pages. Create an outline to facilitate the content migration (see example below).

Sample Content Outline

I. General Library

    a. Facilities and Safety
    b. Materials
    c. Volunteers

II. Reference

    a. Ready Reference
    b. Procedures and Systems
    c. Customer Service

III. Circulation

   a. Procedures
   b. ILS for Circulation
   c. Course Reserves
   d. Interlibrary Loan

IV. Technology

   a. Troubleshooting
   b. Wi-fi
   c. Printers
   d. Phone System
   e. Equipment/Systems

Once the basic outline is created, each content owner will need to add details to each area that specifies how information is grouped and organized. The content owners will determine if each piece of content is large enough to warrant its own page on the WordPress site. The WordPress site shouldn't have an overwhelming amount of pages, but pages should not be so long that users are forced to endlessly scroll through to find what they need.

This project also provides an opportunity to perform a content inventory and update. It will be a priority for content owners to ensure the information is clear, easy-to-understand, and accurate. Instead of writing in long paragraphs, consider using bulleted lists or tables to organize information for the new site. Use a conversational style to make the document easy to read.

Creating Pages

Using the Page tools, create new pages that correspond to the content organization outline the content owners have created. This will serve as the "skeleton" for the site. You do not have to enter content at this time.

1. Create the "top-level" pages first. These pages correspond to the top-level elements in your outline. Refer to the previous content outline. In the example outline, the Roman numerals represent the top-level pages. These are the General Library, Reference,

Circulation, and Technology pages. Create these pages first and then move onto the second-level pages.

2. For the second-level pages it is important to assign the appropriate "Parent" page so the organization of your pages is maintained throughout the site. In the example outline the Facilities and Safety, Materials, and Volunteer pages are the secondary pages under the parent page General Library.

This page creation and organization in the WordPress Dashboard will create the navigation structure of your site.

Setting Up Users

Create user accounts for content owners. In the Users section of the WordPress Dashboard, you can Invite users to your blog using their e-mail addresses. Content owners should be created with the editor role so they are able to create and manage pages. WordPress will automatically send them an e-mail with login information. Other users, who will be able to view the content, will be added during the final steps of site setup.

WordPress allows you to set roles for each person who will contribute to the site. Some of these roles include the following:

- Administrator—has access to create, edit, and publish content and is able to manage user accounts. Note: This account is automatically created when you set up your site.
- Editor—has the ability to publish and manage posts, including those created by other users.
- Author—has the ability to publish and manage his or her own posts.
- Subscriber—has access to view content only.

Set up a project group comprised of the WordPress administrator and content owners to manage the WordPress setup and migration of the content. For this example, let's assume three staff members will coordinate the site organization and content management, representing Circulation, Reference, and Technology. The Technology content owners will also be the WordPress administrator.

Adding Content

By this point you should have a page in WordPress created for each piece of content in your outline. These pages should have parent pages assigned where applicable to ensure the correct organizational structure for the site. The user accounts for content owners should also be set up.

At this point the content owners can begin populating the pages with the content. When creating content for the web in WordPress, use elements such as headers, lists, and tables to make content easy to scan so that staff members are able to locate information easily.

Final Steps and Site Launch

The site administrator(s) can add widgets to customize and enhance the site. In our sample project, we will add the Search and Links widgets to the main page sidebar. These two widgets can be added via the Word-Press Dashboard under Appearance > Widgets.

Once you have added the two widgets, they will automatically appear on your main page. In the WordPress Dashboard, the list of links in the Links widget can be customized using the Links item on the left-hand toolbar.

There are many more customization options available with Word-Press.com, but once your content is migrated by the content owners and you've added a few widgets, your site is now ready to launch. The last step is to create user accounts for all the site users who will be able to view the content. Once you are satisfied with the content, layout, and features of your site, create the user accounts for staff who will need access to the documentation. Users who are not content owners will need to be invited and given the role of viewer. If you are using the blog functionality and want users to be able to create or publish posts, you will need to assign them the role of contributor or author. (See "Support: User Roles," WordPress.com, accessed April 29, 2015, http://en. support.wordpress.com, for more details on WordPress roles.)

When users have access to the site, you may want to provide some basic training and introduction to the online staff handbook. Explain the advantages of using an online platform and demonstrate some of the useful features. Once the staff is using the site on a regular basis, make sure that content owners are maintaining the content so that it remains accurate and relevant for users. After a few months of use, it might also be appropriate to survey the staff as to what other information might be useful to add to the site.

HOW TO MANAGE LIBRARY STATISTICS WITH ZOHO CREATOR

All libraries collect statistics about their collections and resources, but many have issues keeping this information organized. Many organizations end up with unwieldy, messy spreadsheets with multiple contributors that contain this type of data. Using an online, secure database for library statistics is a great alternative to disorganized spreadsheets. Zoho Creator is a web application for managing data. You don't need any special technical skills to implement this solution. It's easy to use, and your finished product is an attractive form that staff members can fill out. Staff will love it because it provides straightforward data entry and administrators will enjoy the slew of reporting options for viewing the data. In this example project, we will examine the steps to collect reference statistics and build insightful reports using Zoho Creator.

Set Up Your First Form

The form-builder in Zoho is a simple drag-and-drop interface. Once you've created a Zoho account, click the gray Create New application button and select the From Scratch option. Give your application the name "Reference Statistics," and click the Create button. Your first form will be autogenerated for you. On the right-hand side of the screen, you can rename the form "Reference Statistics." Now you are ready to start building your form.

All you need to get started is the list of fields you want to track for reference statistics. Let's say we're planning to track the following information for each reference transaction:

- Question—The question the patron asked the library staff member.
- Answer—The answer provided by the staff member.

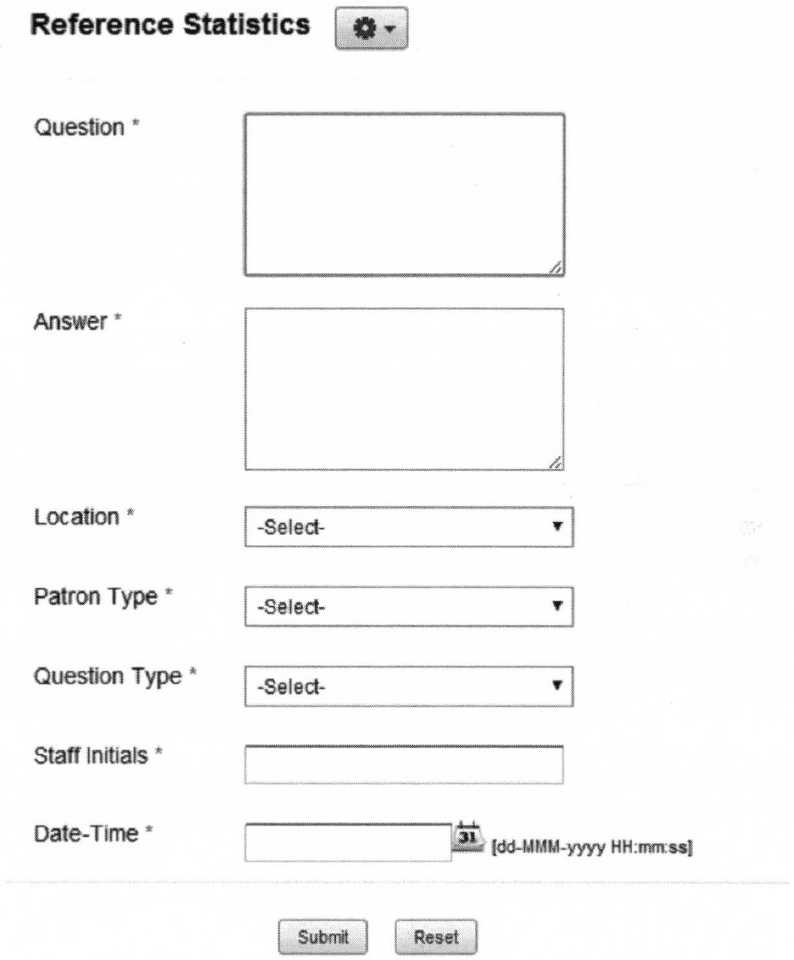

Reference Statistics ⚙▾

Question *

Answer *

Location * -Select- ▾

Patron Type * -Select- ▾

Question Type * -Select- ▾

Staff Initials *

Date-Time * 📅 [dd-MMM-yyyy HH:mm:ss]

Submit   Reset

Figure 5.1. Zoho Creator: form to enter data

- Location—Denotes if the question was asked in person, by phone, or using online chat or e-mail.
- Patron Type—Indicates if the person who asked the question is an adult, a senior, a teen, a child, and so forth.
- Question Type—What type of question is it? Ready reference, research, technology, directions, supplies, and so forth.
- Date/Time of Question—When was the question asked?

- Staff Member Initials—Who on the staff provided the answer?

You will need to decide what kind of field you will use for each data point. Zoho offers a multitude of field types to select from, but don't be overwhelmed. For this first form, you'll only need to use a few different field types: single line, multi-line, drop down, and date-time.

Drag in the following fields:

Figure 5.2. Zoho Creator: form data field types

- Two multi-line fields (for Question and Answer)
- Three drop-down fields (for Location, Patron Type, and Question Type)
- One date-time (for Date/Time)
- One single-line field (for Staff Initials)

Now that you have the fields added to your form, you can rename the fields with the appropriate headings. Click the first Multi-Line field so it is highlighted. The field settings will display on the right-hand side of the screen. Rename each field using the Field Name entry textbox, and decide if you want the field to be mandatory; click the Mandatory checkbox if you want to force users to complete this field when filling out the form. For this form, make all the fields mandatory so you don't have any missing metadata when you build reports later on. If you want to reorder the fields, you can click and drag each field to re-sort.

The final step in building your first form is to populate the drop-down fields. Click into each drop-down field, and add the following options to the Choices entry fields on the right-hand side of the screen.

- Location Choices: In-Person, Phone, Online Chat, and E-mail
- Patron-Type Choices: Adult, Senior, Teen, and Child
- Question-Type Choices: Ready Reference, Research, Technology, Directions, and Supplies

Now your form is ready to be shared and populated by reference staff. Click the green Access This Application button in the upper right corner to preview your form display. You can always return to the administrator interface by clicking the Edit This Application link.

Sharing and Populating Forms with Data

Once you have created your first form, you can start populating your database with relevant content. As the application administrator, you can enter data yourself, but one of the great features of Zoho Creator is that you can easily share the form with staff members to enter in data via a web browser form. Invite contributors to the application through the Dashboard, under Settings > Share. Click the Reference Statistics form checkbox to give the contributors rights to fill out the form. They will then receive an e-mail with a link to the form. They will need to create an account in order to access the form. With the free version of Zoho Creator, you can have an application shared with up to five people (including the administrator). If you need more than five individual accounts, you'll need to upgrade to a paid version of Zoho Creator. Alternatively, you could use a shared e-mail account, such as reference-desk@yourlibrary.com, to access the Reference Statistics form.

When contributors receive a link to the form and create their account, they will be able to fill out the information in the Statistics form. This will populate the database in Zoho Creator. Once staff members have entered in some information, you can create some reports based on the statistics captured via the form.

Creating Reports

Now that data has been entered into the database, you are able to view the data and build reports in Zoho Creator. Zoho Creator offers several types of reports, including pivot tables and charts. Once the reports are built, you can share or download them. After some data has been populated in your Reference Statistics form, a basic report on the entries will appear automatically in your application. This Reference Statistics report behaves similarly to a spreadsheet. You can sort the data by clicking on one of the column headers and also bulk edit entries from this view. The most powerful reports in Zoho Creator are the pivot table reports. Let's build one to see a report that summarizes our data by patron type.

A pivot table report summarizes your data in an easy-to-read grid. Think about what you'd like the report to look like before you begin building. For this pivot table report, we'd like to summarize all the data by patron type. So the question we're asking is, How many questions were asked by each type of patron since we began using this form for reference statistics? On the left of the report, each row of the first column will be the patron type (Adult, Senior, Teen, and Child), and the second column will contain the corresponding number of questions asked by that patron type.

Let's build this report. From the Edit This Application screen, click the Create New icon on the left and select Report. Name the report "Statistics by Patron Type," and select Pivot Table from the Report

Student Type	Question Type	Number of Questions Asked
▼ Master/Grad Student	Careers	2
	Computers	40
	Directions	55
	Guest Login	4
	Other Technology	67
	Printers	109
	Ready Reference/Research Help	1087
	Simmons Technology Referral	17
	Supplies - Staplers Paperclips etc.	27
	Writing/Citation	54
Master/Grad Student Total		1462
▼ Undergrad Student	Careers	3
	Computers	18
	Directions	37
	Guest Login	2
	Other Technology	12
	Printers	59
	Ready Reference/Research Help	227
	Simmons Technology Referral	11
	Supplies - Staplers Paperclips etc.	27
	Writing/Citation	10
Undergrad Student Total		406
Grand Total		1868

Figure 5.3. Pivot table report summarizing reference desk transactions

Type drop-down. Set the Report Based On to the Reference Statistics form. Don't be overwhelmed by the pivot table report builder—we won't need to use all the options for this report. Remember we want the rows to be the patron type, and the data to be the number of questions answered. This will provide a nice summary to show the types of patrons who most frequently ask questions at the reference desk. Drag the Patron Type field to the Rows area of the report builder. Then drag in any other field to the Data area. This will generate a report showing a count of how many questions were answered for each type of patron. Click the Save button when you are done and then the Access This Application button to see the final report.

You may want to build these pivot reports for each of your drop-down fields to easily view reference questions by location and question type as well. Another type you might consider building in the future is to summarize the data by date/time (or day of the week), which can help with staffing decisions. Once you're comfortable building a pivot table report you can also add filters to give more control to the report viewer. Using the statistics collection form, basic report, and pivot table reports will provide you with valuable insights into trends related to reference desk service.

HOW TO PROVIDE PROGRAMMING, INSTRUCTION, AND REFERENCE TO GROUPS OF OFF-SITE PATRONS

There are numerous free, easy-to-use, virtual communication tools available online. Tools such as AnyMeeting.com and Join.Me can be used to provide services to patrons who are unable to visit the library in person. You don't need any special equipment to use these services, though they can be enhanced with a webcam or microphone, hardware your library might already own. These tools enable you to host webinars, share your screen, set up telephone conference calls, and communicate with participants through the web. All of the interactivity takes place within the browser, and participants never have to install anything on their machine. You will be able to teach large groups of participants or provide more focused one-on-one instruction to off-site patrons by making use of these tools.

Before setting up any virtual meetings (also known as webinars) you should practice with the tool you'll make use of. Although these tools are very straightforward to use, you should familiarize yourself in order to make communication easier, rather than complicate it. In order for the patron to have a successful experience, take time before the meeting to rehearse with the software, understand the interface's layout, and master the features you want to use with participants. Be prepared for questions from the participants about using the tool, and be ready to troubleshoot issues that may come up. You may even want to host a mock meeting with staff members in order to practice for the real event. Like in-person instruction or programming, the participant's experience will be greatly improved if you do sufficient preparation and are able to master the tool you're using.

Setting Up AnyMeeting

Imagine you want to broadcast a library workshop to patrons who are unable to come into the building. Using the presentation tool AnyMeeting.com, you will be able to share a PowerPoint presentation, demonstrate actions on your computer's screen, and facilitate discussion with your participants. The free, ad-supported account from AnyMeeting.com allows you to broadcast your meeting to up to two hundred people.

Create an account via AnyMeeting.com using your e-mail address to get started. Once you have an account with AnyMeeting.com, you can practice with the interface and try out the functionality by immediately starting a meeting. The site also allows you to schedule meetings in advance and invite attendees. For now, though, launch a meeting to test out the basic functionality, since it's important to familiarize yourself with the tool before holding an actual meeting. Note that the basic functionality might be limited without meeting attendees.

The first option you'll be prompted to choose is how your audio will be shared between attendees. If you have a reliable, fast Internet connection and a microphone, it is easier to use the audio through your computer. Although many computers have built-in microphones, the audio quality will be better for your participants if you use an external microphone, either freestanding or connected to a headset. When using the computer for audio, you can mute yourself by clicking on your name in the list of participants. If you're unsure of the reliability of your Internet connection, you will probably want to use a conference phone number to dial in to present. Your audio will be best if you use an audio headset that connects to your phone for lengthier meetings. The hands-free mic will also let you be more comfortable during your presentation. Virtual meetings can sometimes be plagued by audio issues, so be sure to test out the different configurations before holding any actual meeting.

After you select the audio option, you will enter the meeting. The browser will automatically detect if you have a webcam and will ask if you want to share your webcam feed with participants. Using a webcam is not required by AnyMeeting.com, but the meeting will be more engaging for attendees if they can see your face while you present.

Understanding the AnyMeeting Interface

The AnyMeeting screen might seem slightly overwhelming at first glance, but once you take a few moments to orient yourself, it is easy to understand.

The first thing you should notice, and then ignore, is the advertisements that display on the right side of the screen. You might want to alert your attendees that these advertisements will cycle throughout

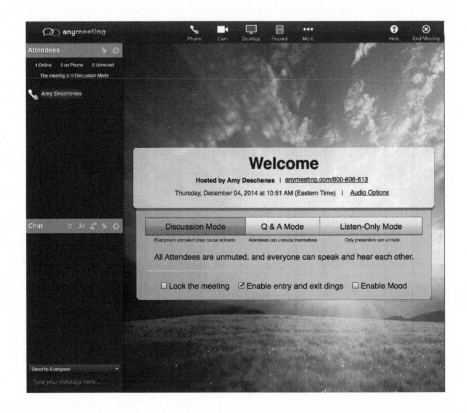

Figure 5.4. AnyMeeting Start Screen

your meeting and explain that you are able to hold these virtual meetings for free because the system is ad supported.

Notice the gray box in the center of the screen. This box contains meeting details, including a link to the meeting that can be shared with attendees; the link looks like anymeeting.com/XXX-XXX-XXX. Attendees can also be added to the meeting by sending them an e-mail invitation using the Invite link at the top of the screen.

The gray box in the center of the screen also contains important meeting setup options. There are three options for audio sharing and attendee participation. Consider what kind of program you're hosting before selecting an option. If you select the Listen-Only mode where all participants are muted except for the presenter, participants can always use the chat to participate. If your library is new to hosting webinars, the Listen-Only mode is the easiest to start with. You can always get back to these options from the Meeting Options link at the top of the screen. At the bottom of the gray box, you can also set the meeting as Locked, meaning no more attendees can enter, as well as enabling a ding signaling when another person joins the meeting.

The core AnyMeeting functionality is displayed at the top center of the screen. Here is where you can configure your webcam and microphone settings. There are also options to create public and private meeting notes, and set your mood. Most important are the options listed under the Share option at the top of the screen. Use the Share options to show your desktop to meeting attendees to demonstrate something, play a YouTube video, upload a pdf or PowerPoint document, and run audience polls.

Audio and Interactivity Options in AnyMeeting

Enabling two-way communication with your participants is essential to an effective online meeting. Even if you are holding a Listen Only–style meeting, you should still let attendees communicate using the chat option on the lower left. Attendees can send messages either to the group or only to the presenter. You may want to invite attendees to send in questions at certain points during your presentation, or let them know you'll watch the chat feed during the whole meeting—though this definitely takes some practice since you can lose your train of thought if you're trying to keep up with the chat throughout your entire presentation.

Using polling during your meeting is a great way to collect organized feedback from your participants. You can set up polls before the meeting begins and then use the Polls button to start voting at certain points during the presentation. The polls keep participants engaged and also give them a sense of the outlooks of other attendees. Note that when a poll is ongoing, it takes up the majority of the screen space and cannot be minimized.

After familiarizing yourself with AnyMeeting and perhaps holding a trial meeting, you're ready to hold your first webinar. From the AnyMeeting administrative interface, select the option to Schedule a Meeting. Complete the schedule information first. If you're planning on holding an hour presentation, you might consider bookending the meeting with extra time so that there is ample time for setup and answering any troubleshooting questions participants may have. You cannot have more than one meeting scheduled during a specific time slot.

Organizing Meeting Participants

There are two options for organizing participants when you advertise your online meeting. You can advertise the link to the meeting as part of the promotional materials (e.g., "Join this meeting from your web browser on Monday, June 2, at 2:00 p.m. by going to anymeeting.com/ XXX-XXX-XXX"), which would make it easy for anyone to join the meeting without being invited by the meeting organizer. Alternatively, if you want to force participants to sign up in advance, you could have some kind of sign-up form where people express their intent to attend. Once you have a list of attendees, you can invite them to the meeting from the meeting scheduling interface.

If you have multiple presenters, it is important to make sure they are added to the specific presenter list because they will receive slightly different instructions for logging into the meeting. You can always add additional attendees or presenters later on. Finally, enter the details about the meeting into the e-mail message area, and select the final meeting options. When you finish the meeting invitation, you can click the Schedule Meeting Now button to immediately send the invitations, or the Next button to configure more options about the meeting such as a registration form or survey.

Participants will have the option of calling in to listen to the audio or using their computer speakers. If you want participants to speak during the meeting, they will need to have a microphone attached to their computer if they aren't using their phone for audio. Using the chat feature in AnyMeeting might be a good alternative for taking basic questions from participants rather than coordinating audio setup for all participants. If you enable audio for all participants, you may end up with unwanted echoes in the background of your meeting.

Start small with AnyMeeting, and give participants the opportunity to provide feedback about the virtual meeting experience. Holding a virtual meeting is a very different experience than presenting programming or instruction to a room full of people. Even when there are no technical issues, it can be difficult to understand how engaged your audience is. It can also be distracting to the audience when there are technical issues. However, making sure you are comfortable with the tool you're using to provide the webinar can go a long way to reduce technical problems and confusion. For more information on creating effective webinars, check out the book *Content Rules: How to Create Killer Blogs, Podcasts, Videos, Ebooks, Webinars (and More) That Engage Customers and Ignite Your Business* by Ann Handley.

HOW TO USE SCREEN SHARING FOR REMOTE REFERENCE

If you don't want to use a robust webinar solution, such as AnyMeeting, you can use a simpler screen-sharing tool to demonstrate anything on your computer to an online user. Using Join.Me, you can present your screen with anyone through the web browser and share audio as well. Join.Me is simpler than AnyMeeting and is a great option if you're looking for a basic screen-sharing tool, instead of a robust online meeting solution.

As a presenter, you will need to install a program on your computer in order to share your screen and start the conference, but the viewer does not need to download anything or create an account. This option is best for quick demos with individuals or small groups (less than ten people). Join.Me is great for walking patrons through a process during a reference transaction or holding an online reference appointment. As when introducing any new technology tool, it is important to practice with the interface in order to get comfortable before holding your first meeting.

To get started with Join.Me, you'll need to download the program from the Join.Me website; patrons will not need to download anything to participate in the meeting. After installing Join.Me and launching the app, you'll see a small widget attached to the top of your desktop. From the Join.Me widget, you can launch a screen-sharing session immediately; there is no functionality to schedule these sessions in advance. You can start the screen-sharing session by using the orange Share button. After clicking the Share button, you screen sharing will begin and the widget will display the Join.Me controls. Invite others to view your screen by sending them the link that is displayed in the widget:

join.me/XXX-XXX-XXX. They will be able to view your screen by navigating to this link in their browser. The largest, center button in the widget lets you pause desktop sharing. When you pause desktop sharing, the image on the viewer's end will appear frozen until you resume sharing. Once a participant joins, you can use the other buttons to start an audio call, chat using the chat box, and share mouse control with the participants.

Let's imagine you are on the phone with a female patron trying to explain how to load an e-book from the library onto her e-reader. Explaining a computer process can be confusing and frustrating without any real-time visual accompaniment. If you have installed Join.Me on your computer, you can launch a screen-sharing session instantly. After you launch the session, you will see the Join.Me link to the meeting. You can automatically copy the link to the clipboard or send it via e-mail by clicking it. Send the link to the patron via e-mail or online chat. You could also read it to her if you're on the phone with her and she can type it in the browser. Once she has accessed the link via her web browser, she will see your screen.

You will see a message on your screen when the patron successfully accesses the Join.Me session. After demonstrating the e-book loading functionality to your patron, you can pass control by using the ". . ." button and selecting Share Mouse Control. She can then control the screen via the browser with her own mouse. Sharing control of your screen makes walking someone through a computer process much simpler. Ask her to try out the e-book functionality on your screen so you can watch her perform the process and provide any tips while she's practicing it.

Both AnyMeeting and Join.Me make presenting to and communicating with online patrons much easier. However, before embarking on any project with online patrons, it is important to make sure the tools you implement are appropriate for your users. While AnyMeeting makes sense for a large group presentation, Join.Me is much easier for quick-hit-style demonstrations. Depending on the information technology (IT) setup at your institution, other tools, such as Google Hangouts or Zoho Meeting, might be more appropriate. Take the time to select the appropriate tool and master using it before offering it as a service enhancement to your community.

IMPLEMENTING A SCALABLE E-RESOURCES MANAGEMENT SYSTEM

This project has a few more requirements than the others we've looked at so far, but setting up this open-source system for managing e-resources is doable, even with little technical background. The open-source electronic-resources management system CORAL provides a flexible and scalable interface for managing e-resources.

Let's imagine your library has been managing e-resources via an Excel spreadsheet and wants to implement something more robust and accessible. CORAL is a fantastic solution because it is free and has thorough documentation and an active user community. We're going to focus on creating an online database of resources and organizations in this example. You can take the system even further by utilizing the Licensing and Usage Statistics modules to manage files you upload; however, those modules won't be covered in this example.

Using CORAL is a great, low-maintenance option for managing e-resources. There are many benefits to using it, including the following:

- the ability to add to and edit your e-resources metadata from any computer with an Internet connection;
- the option to upload license agreements so you can access and review those from anywhere;
- the ability to create staff accounts so other library staff members can view statistics and metadata, without having the ability to edit records;
- the alerts feature, which allows you to automatically notify staff when a resource license or subscription is up for renewal;
- a system that centralizes record-keeping for all e-resources your library manages (it will help reduce data redundancy and formalize e-resources record-keeping); and
- a highly customizable system in which you can include as much, or as little, information as you need to.

There are two main segments to successfully migrating to CORAL. First, you'll need to set up the system on your library's web server; and second, you'll need to enter your databases licenses into the system. Libraries of all sizes use this software, so don't think you don't have the human resources to support it. If you have a little bit of technical know-how and are comfortable following detailed directions, you can set up this system.

Setting Up CORAL

You can install the system on a web server you host yourself or via a hosting service you subscribe to. Most libraries with websites already have some kind of web space, and this application can be installed alongside other sites. But smaller libraries may not. If you're one of them, you might consider signing up with a web host such as A Small Orange (www.asmallorange.com) for less than seventy dollars per year to host the program for you. CORAL requires a web server with MySQL and PHP, where it can be installed; however, most web hosts offer this type of environment. It is easy to set up even if you have no prior experience with these technologies.

Before setting up any new system, especially an open-source one, it is extremely important to read through all of the documentation. I cannot stress this point enough! Your life will be much easier if you familiarize yourself with the setup requirements and system quirks before diving into the setup. Luckily, the designers of CORAL have provided excellent technical documentation to support the installation (see "CORAL—Main: CORAL Technical Documentation," GitHub, last updated April 14, 2014, https://github.com).

First, download the most recent CORAL files from the CORAL website. This will download all of the web files the application needs to run—think of it as downloading a prebuilt website. There will be HTML, JavaScript, and PHP files. Don't worry; you won't need to modify any code directly! There are two ways to install CORAL: through the web browser walk-through or manually. It is recommended to use the web browser installer since that will check to make sure your setup includes all the requirements CORAL needs; that way you won't need to edit any code. Upload the folder you downloaded from the CORAL website to your web space using an FTP program such as FileZilla (https://filezilla-project.org).

When you have uploaded the CORAL files to your web space, you are ready to begin the installation. CORAL contains several modules that need to be installed individually. Navigate to [yourwebspacename]/

coral to see the CORAL main menu. None of the links will work yet because you still need to run the setup in order to configure the database. Install each module by typing in [yourwebspacename]/coral/modulename/install. For example, if your library's web space was www.any townlibrary.gov, you would navigate to www.anytownlibrary.gov/coral/auth/install to install the authorization module.

You do not need to install every module. It is a good idea to read through the documentation before installing to decide which modules are appropriate for your library. However, if you choose to install all modules, follow this order: authorization, resources, organizations, licensing, and usage. Follow the instructions and prompts on this installer page to configure the system. This setup will create the CORAL database and underlying tables to hold all of your e-resources data. There is much more you can do to customize your CORAL installation, but this setup will provide you with basic system functionality.

Setting Up User Accounts

Once you've set up the system, you'll need to create user accounts for the staff members who will need access to the system. You can log in to the system using the user credentials (different from the database credentials) you created during the setup. By using an administrator account, you are able to create other user accounts from any module. Click the Admin link at the top of the screen to manage user accounts and create accounts for each staff member who will need access to the system. There are three types of accounts: admin, add/edit, and view. Admin accounts give the user access to all of the system settings, add/edit accounts are for managing data entry, and view accounts are for staff members who need access to the system but won't be modifying data. You may want to create accounts for staff members who will manage e-resources (add/edit account) and also for those who need to review license agreements and e-resource statistics (view account).

Configuring Settings

Before you begin entering your resource and vendor information, it is best to configure the administrative settings for each module. Some of the fields in CORAL are drop-down menus populated by the information you enter in the administrative setup. Start with the Organizations module. Here you will create the vendor records for your resources. The vendor records will contain information about your contacts at the organization, along with any related administrative accounts for this vendor. If you set up organization records first, you can then assign them to resource records in the Resources module. Below is an example of the relationship between an Organization record and multiple resource records.

Organization record: EBSCO

Resource records: Academic Search Complete, Business Source Premier, Newspaper Source, and SocIndex

In the Resources module, you'll want to at least create some workflow/user group, resource format, resource type, and subject options. There are many other fields you can add to resource records using the administrative interface, but start with the basics. The workflow/user group options allow you to track the process of purchasing and activating each resource; you are providing the resource with a status within CORAL with this field. The other options you set up in the administrative area will often be the groupings you use for reporting. Consider the audience for this data and how the information will be reported on in the future.

Populating E-Resources into CORAL and Sharing the Data

Once the administrative options are configured, you can enter resource records into the system.

In addition to tracking resource acquisitions and storing platform information all in one place, CORAL is a great tool for sharing resource information with the entire library staff. If you have set up view accounts for staff members, they are able to log in and view information about the resources they care about. Depending on how you've set up the resource fields in the administrative area, you will have certain search and filter options on the main page of the Resources module. Library staff can use these list filters to only see resources with a certain format or for a specific subject area. The system makes it easier to troubleshoot resources and provides easy access to vendor contacts, accessible from any browser.

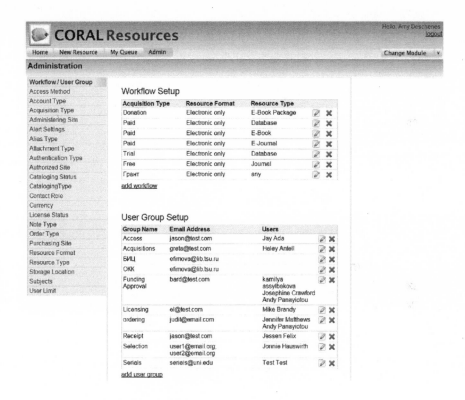

Figure 5.5. CORAL Admin module

As with any library system, CORAL is only as good as the data that is in it. Once the system is set up and the data are entered initially, there needs to be a maintenance plan so the data doesn't become obsolete. Maintaining the data in CORAL might be something that is done frequently, if you are adding resources on a regular basis, or an activity that is only done once a year, to coincide with renewals.

One of the strengths of CORAL as an open-source solution is there is a smart, active user community enabled through a listserv. You can join the list "by sending an email to listserv@listserv.nd.edu. Leave the subject line blank and include 'SUBSCRIBE CORAL-ERM Your Name' in the body; ex. SUBSCRIBE CORAL-ERM John Smith" ("About CORAL," CORAL, accessed April 30, 2015, http://coral-erm. org). There is also a steering committee for the software made up of members from Texas A&M, North Carolina State University, University of Notre Dame, Duke Medical Center Library, and Calvin College.

If you have any issues setting up the software or getting started, the community is quick to respond and exceedingly helpful.

USING GOOGLE FORMS TO MANAGE PURCHASE REQUESTS

Google Forms makes it easy to collect information from patrons about any topic. Libraries are using Google Forms to collect feedback on programming and log reference statistics, and to keep track of student worker hours. One useful implementation is to use Google Forms to organize purchase requests from patrons. By offering a form on the library website, you will have a simple, singular point where patrons can communicate what items they would like to see added to the collection. The form can be embedded into your library's website and linked to on appropriate pages. Once a patron submits the form, each request is added as a row in an online spreadsheet that staff members can use to inform purchase decisions.

Planning Your Forms

Consider what information you want to collect from patrons when they fill out this request form before you begin building the form. You might consider including some introductory text about the library's collection-development policy before the entry fields. You'll also want to determine if there are any fields that are "required," which is usually denoted with an asterisk in online forms. Let's assume we're building a form for a large university library and we want to collect the following information from patrons:

- Title *
- Author
- Publisher
- Publication year
- Patron name *
- Patron e-mail address *
- Patron type (undergraduate, graduate, faculty, staff, or library staff)

- Date needed by
- Special instructions

Consider how you want the data to appear in the spreadsheet of results. There are some fields that might be better as drop-downs or multiple choice instead of blank text fields. This will make filtering results easier. Other fields, such as author and patron name, might need to be broken into two fields: last name and first name. This way your list of results will be uniform. Keep the names of fields user-friendly. Patron Name might sound unfamiliar to a user, so use something more familiar, such as Your Last Name instead. You may also want to add some notes under certain questions to help patrons fill out the form. For example, under the Special Instructions field, you may want to add something such as "Use this field to indicate if you would like the item in physical or electronic format." Once you have your notes on these form details, you're ready to begin building the form.

Building the Forms

You'll need to create a Google Drive account in order to create a Google Form. If you have a Gmail account, you will automatically have access to Google Drive. Visit http://drive.google.com in your browser to create your first form. Under the red Create button, you will see the option for Form. After clicking the Form option, you will be prompted to enter a title for your form and select a theme. You can then begin adding items to your form.

There are basic form elements such as choose from a list, multiple choice, and Likert scale questions, but for the majority of the questions for this type of form, you can simply add the text option. This will create an open-ended-style blank field in the form where the patron can enter information. Click the Required checkbox to indicate when the field is required. Don't forget to add help text to questions where appropriate. This text will provide patrons with guidance as they fill out the form. After you have added your fields, set the confirmation page options. You can set certain options for the form behavior and enter a custom submissions success message. Once you are happy with your draft, click the View Live Form button to see what the form will look like to patrons.

Publishing the Forms

You now have a form where patrons can submit purchase requests. There are a few ways to provide access to the form. From the form editor page, select the File > Send Form menu option to see a link to your live form; you can now provide this link on your website. However, it is more seamless if you embed the form on your library website, so it feels more integrated with your website. Integrating the form is simple, and though it does require working with a bit of HTML code, you won't need to edit any code directly, only copy and paste. From the File > Send Form option, click the Embed button. The Embed information will display. The form is included in the iframe HTML element in this window. You can set the dimensions of the form using the fields at the bottom of the box. Once you have the correct width and height, copy the iframe tag and paste this entire tag into the page on your website where you want your form to display.

Now you have a working purchase request form on your website. If you go back to the main Google Drive page, you will see two files, the Form you've created and a spreadsheet file that will hold form submissions. Each time the form is submitted, the data is entered into a row in this spreadsheet. The first column is a time stamp of when the form entry was submitted. You can add additional columns to the end of this spreadsheet without them showing up on the form. This way you can enter in notes about each request. Google Sheets also provides tools similar to Microsoft Excel for filtering, sorting, and hiding/showing entries. You can also share this spreadsheet with other Google Drive users by using the blue Share button and entering their e-mail address.

Using Google Forms will help you organize your purchase requests, but one more tweak will make it even better—adding e-mail notifications. Instead of having to periodically check the Google Sheet to see if there are any new requests, you can set up the spreadsheet to send an e-mail each time a new request is added to the form. Select the Tools > Notification Rules menu option. Set the option to send an e-mail anytime a "user submits a form," and decide if you want the e-mail to be sent immediately or in "daily digest" format, meaning you will only get one e-mail a day with a summary of all the responses. The Notification Rules settings will only send you the notification e-mail saying that someone has submitted the form; it does not include the content of the submission. You can accomplish sending an e-mail with the form submission data by using a script in Google Forms (see the Google e-mail form at www.labnol.org).

PROMOTING A LIBRARY EVENT THROUGH IN-PERSON AND ONLINE ADVERTISING

Your library can host fascinating events and teach the best workshops, but if no one notices your advertising, your programming will never be well attended. In order to reach the most patrons possible, consider using a combination of dynamic e-mails and easy-to-create, in-person signage to promote events in your library. Using some free online tools to create posters and an e-mail campaign for your events will save you time and create an eye-catching advertisement.

Setting Up an E-mail Marketing Campaign with MailChimp

MailChimp is a great tool to create professional-looking e-mails, manage contacts, and track engagement results. You are able to customize the content, format, and branding of these e-mails to match any of your library's existing marketing materials. E-mails will look great, and you can make sure your interested patrons are always in-the-know once they're subscribed to your mailing list. Let's assume this is your first e-mail campaign. You'll need to collect interested subscriber e-mails and design an e-mail template to get started. The Forever Free account allows you to have up to two thousand subscribers and send twelve thousand e-mails a month. The first thing to do is to create a user account from the MailChimp home page (www.mailchimp.com).

Creating a Form to Collect Subscriber Information

Once you have confirmed your MailChimp account via your e-mail address, you're ready to begin creating a form where patrons can sign up for your e-mails. From the MailChimp dashboard, select the Create List menu item; then click the Create button in the upper right section. This list is the list of e-mail addresses to which your e-mails will be distributed. Even if you don't have e-mail addresses yet, you still need to set up a list so you can create a form where patrons can provide their e-mail address in order to subscribe. Give your list a name, and set the defaults for the default "from name" that will display in your e-mails, along with the default "from" e-mail. The "from" e-mail is the address that patrons will use if they choose to respond to one of the e-mails you send via MailChimp. Finally, select the new subscriber notification settings. Choose if you want to receive an e-mail each time a new person signs up ("one by one") or a daily e-mail summary of new subscribers ("daily digest"). Enter the e-mail address you'd like these new sign-up notifications to be sent to. You can also customize the confirmation message that is sent to subscribers when they join the e-mail list.

Setting Up Your First E-mail Campaign

Now that you've configured a list, you need to create a form where patrons can sign up for your promotional e-mails. From the dashboard, navigate to the Lists area using the menu on the left. Click on the list that you just created, and select the Signup Forms link. There are options for creating general forms, which generate a URL you can provide to patrons where they can go to sign up; embedded forms that generate some basic HTML that you can paste inside a page on your website; and form integrations that you can use to build a form for WordPress. Let's assume we will be inserting this sign-up form onto a page on the library's website. Choose the Embedded Form option, and you will see the Embedded Form Code page. The default classic form will display. You can tweak the form using the options on the left, but there is nothing that absolutely needs to be changed. All you need to do is copy the HTML in the "Copy/paste onto your site" box and paste this code somewhere in your website.

Now that you have a working form, patrons will be able to sign up for your e-mail list. You might consider promoting your e-mail list via signage or social media to encourage patrons to sign up. Now that patrons are signing up for your e-mail list, you can create your first campaign. In the MailChimp dashboard, select the Campaigns option from the navigation on the left; then click the Create Campaign button in the upper right corner. You will see a list of campaigns to pick from. Select Regular Ol' Campaign to create your first e-mail.

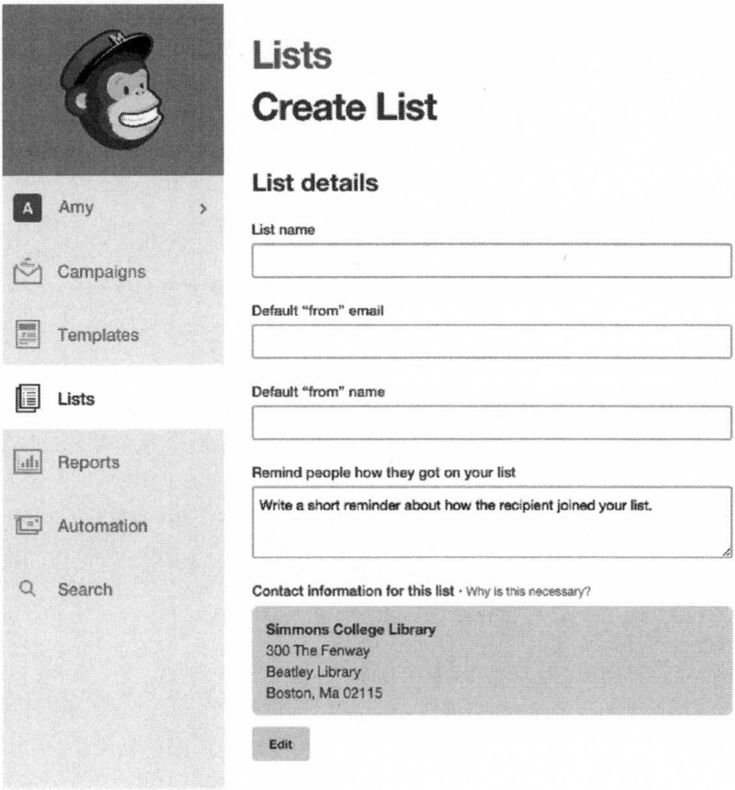

Lists
Create List

List details

List name

Default "from" email

Default "from" name

Remind people how they got on your list

Write a short reminder about how the recipient joined your list.

Contact information for this list · Why is this necessary?

Simmons College Library
300 The Fenway
Beatley Library
Boston, Ma 02115

Edit

A Amy   >

Campaigns

Templates

Lists

Reports

Automation

Q Search

Figure 5.6. MailChimp: setting up a list

MailChimp will now walk you through setting up your e-mail campaign. There are four main settings: Recipients, Setup, Template, and Design. In each section you will select the options for this particular e-mail campaign. After you have configured each section, click the gray Next button in the lower right corner of the page.

Recipients

Select the "Send to entire list" option. This will send your campaign to everyone who has signed up via the online form.

Setup

Fill out the details for your campaign under Campaign Info including the following fields:

- Name your campaign—this name will appear in your MailChimp administrative interface.
- E-mail subject—what recipients will see as the subject of your e-mail.
- "From" name—the "friendly" name for your library or organization.
- "From" e-mail address—the e-mail address assigned to the From field in your e-mail. It is best to use a shared organizational e-mail address rather than an individual's e-mail account.

For all other details, you can use the default selections unless you want to explore tweaking the settings further.

Template

You will see many options to pick from under the Basic templates page. Select the Left Sidebar template using the Select button next to the template picture. You can see a full-screen preview of the template by clicking the magnifying glass while hovering over the template. We will build a basic newsletter welcome letter, with links to important library links on the left sidebar using this template. Once you select a template, the Design window will open.

Design

First customize the content in your e-mail. You can customize the images, text, and links of the template by clicking on each section of the template. When you click an element, a basic editor will appear on the right side of the screen. Here you can customize the content and font display for your e-mail. You can also drag in images and drop them directly onto the template to personalize the e-mail.

Finally, personalize the design of the e-mail by clicking the Design tab on the right side of the screen. You will see subheadings where you can customize each element of the e-mail such as the header, sidebar, body, and footer. If your library website has a color scheme or a marketing color scheme, you may want to draw from those colors so there is a cohesive feeling with other library branding. Once you are happy with the design elements, you will be ready to send the e-mail to recipients.

Sending Your First Campaign to Subscribers

After finalizing the design of your e-mail, you're ready to send the e-mail to subscribers. On the Confirm page, you will see a checklist of items related to the e-mail campaign settings you've selected. Review the settings and make sure everything is correct. You can then schedule your e-mail to be sent at a future date and time or send the e-mail immediately using the Send button at the bottom of the page. If you click the Send button, you'll get one more confirmation page asking you if you're sure you're ready to send your e-mail. Click the Send Now button to distribute your first e-mail.

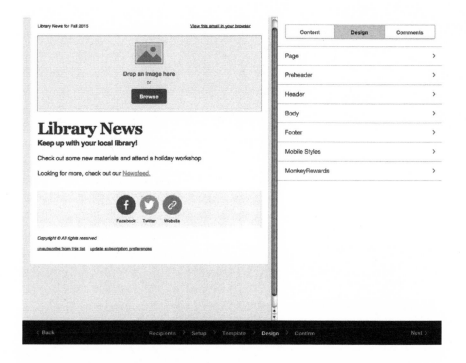

Figure 5.7. MailChimp: design form

Reviewing E-mail Statistics and Creating Other Campaigns

Now that you've sent your first e-mail, you can track recipient engagement through the Reports page on the MailChimp administrator interface. Click the Reports item in the MailChimp administrator interface to see how many subscribers opened your e-mail and if recipients clicked on any links you included in your e-mails. These statistics are a great way to determine whether your e-mail marketing is effective.

One of the features of MailChimp is that you do not have to re-create the design every time you create a campaign. If you want to replicate a campaign but have the option to edit the content and layout, click the Campaigns option on the MailChimp administrator page to view your first campaign. Then click the drop-down arrow on the right, and select the Replicate option. This will create a new campaign with the same settings as your first campaign. You're then able to customize the settings of this second campaign, but keep whatever elements you want from the first.

After you've created your first e-mail campaign, you might consider creating a schedule for distributing these promotional e-mails. Perhaps your library could create a monthly newsletter highlighting news, events, and important information. You could also use MailChimp to promote specific events for certain populations.

CREATING MARKETING POSTERS WITH POSTEROVEN

To promote your events in physical spaces, you'll want to create some professional-looking marketing materials. Eye-catching posters will help promote your events and increase interest in your library. If you don't have access or time to manage building a poster from a blank Microsoft Word document, PosterOven offers fantastic and free poster templates via an online interface—you don't even need to create an account. It's very easy to create professional-looking signs using this tool. Click the Get Started button on the PosterOven.com home page to create your first sign.

The first step is to select a template from the available options. Click the Choose Template link, and select the Ripped Orange template. You will then need to customize the content sections. Enter your own header, text box, middle bar, and bottom bar content; then click the Next button. If you want to keep the social media links, you can customize them here. Otherwise, you can click the X to remove the social media codes from the poster. For this poster, let's just keep the "Facebook" item and customize the link so it points to your organization's Facebook page. You may want to add a link to sign up for e-mails, using the link to the form you created with MailChimp. Click on the Next button to finish your sign.

The final step is to download your poster, but you may want to customize the elements to make the sign the best it can be. Click the Customize Design link to see more options for customization. If you want to change the base color of the sign, you'll need to obtain the hex code for the color; you can use a site such as http://html-color-codes.info to find the hex code for the color you want. There are also options to change the graphics, but this will distort the layout of the poster—be cautious if you choose to modify.

Finally, you can upload a logo and change the text color by selecting the Customize Text Colors radio button under Custom Text Colors. You are then able to select different colors for each text area. Try to keep the color scheme to three colors or less so the poster is clear and easy to read. All that is left to do after you're finished with the customizations is to download and print your poster.

CREATING AN HTML5 RESPONSIVE WEBSITE—NO DESIGN EXPERIENCE REQUIRED!

Although we know it is important to keep up with the latest web standards and trends, there can often be competing priorities and no time to learn the latest development best practices. If your library website needs a redesign, but you don't have the time, money, or human resources to design and code a site from the ground up, you can use a free HTML5 framework to build your new, responsive website. Using an HTML5 framework is a great way to get a fantastic website up and running quickly, without handwriting any code. It's a good idea to be a bit familiar with HTML and CSS markup, but you'll only need to make minor edits to the code and be able to add content. You will need to be ready with your content to populate the template, but there is no designing or intense coding. Let's explore how to use an HTML5 template to get a responsive website up and running quickly.

You'll need to first download the HTML5 template from the W3 Layouts website (www.w3layouts.com). Search for the Public Library template. You can then view a demo site and download the template. After downloading the zip file, unzip it and upload the resulting "web" folder to your web space. Open a browser window and navigate to [yourwebspace]/web to view the template. Try resizing the browser window to see the responsive action. This site will look great regardless of whether the user is on a mobile phone, tablet, or large desktop. The site will automatically adjust to fit the screen in the best way. Now we need to tweak the content a bit so it represents your organization.

Even if you're not an HTML/CSS expert—don't worry. Some cursory web markup knowledge is enough to customize this site. Let's start by updating the navigation and page titles. Open the index.html to edit the navigation. You will see the navigation in an unordered list near line 47. Move the Services link to be the second item in the list. Rename the About page "Events" and update the href="about.html" link to be href="events.html" instead. Rename the Staff page "Kids and Teens," and update the href="staff.html" link to be href="kids+teens.html" instead. You will need to open the other HTML files and update the navigation in each of these files as well. Do not change the "active" class in the HTML or the tabs won't display properly. Finally, change the actual file names of the about.html file to events.html, and rename the staff.html file to kids+teens.html.

If you are ambitious with coding you may consider creating a universal header file, but this is not a required step. This universal header file would store all the HTML head tag information, the main navigation structure, the search box, and social links. The benefit of creating this type of file is that when you make a change, you only need to update one file, instead of having to update multiple files with the same information. Depending on your web server, you may use a server side include, PHP include, or JavaScript include command to set up this kind of universal file. (Read about one of the most common include methods, via PHP at "PHP 5 Include Files," W3schools.com, accessed April 30, 2015, www.w3schools.com.)

Now we'll work on customizing the home-page content. You'll want to replace the three photos in the slider at the top of the page with

Figure 5.8. W3 Layouts: Public Library HTML5 template

images of your own patrons using your library. Remember to get appropriate permissions before uploading someone's photo to your website. An easy way out is to use photos of your library space, but seeing people on a website is much more engaging for the user. Once you have selected your three photos, upload them to the Images folder inside the Web folder of your site. Then, in the index.html file, update the "data-thumb=" selector with the file names of the images you uploaded. After you've updated those images, find the image of the man in the gray suit and remove it from the page (or replace it with a more appropriate image if you'd like). Save the file and preview the web page in your browser. You will now see your own photos in the image slider.

We also should simplify the content on the home page; it is a bit overwhelming as is. Let's remove everything after the What Our Customers Say section (which we will update with our own content). In the index.html, remove everything after the div containing What Our Customers Say until the footer tags. Now when you refresh the page, it will be much shorter. The last two things to change to the home-page layout are the search box and the social media links. You'll want to find the area of code that contains the search box and replace the search box with the code for your library's search (you can probably get this from your integrated library system [ILS] or discovery system vendor). Finally, customize the links to social media sites you maintain, and remove the icons for any social media sites that are listed but that you do not use.

The other page that needs some layout customization is the Contact page. In the contact.html file, delete the div tag containing the contact form. We also need to update the Google Maps link and image in this page. To get an accurate iframe tag with the map information for your library, navigate to Google Maps and enter in your library's full address. Click the gear icon at the bottom of the map, and select Share and Embed Map—a new window will pop up. Under the Embed Map option, you will see the iframe tag you can paste into your contact.html page, replacing the default map iframe tag.

The most important part of this project is updating the content. Much of the language that comes with the template is business focused and will need to be updated. On the home page, consider replacing the What Our Customers Say with a Note from the Director, or What People Think, highlighting some positive feedback your library has received from patrons. You will also need to replace the stock images with pictures that highlight your library's events, services, and resources. Don't forget to customize the page title and main header with your library's name. With those few minor code changes, you should already have a good-looking, responsive site. Looking for more tips on responsive design? Check out Jason Clark's book on the topic *Responsive Web Design in Practice*, also available in the Library Technology Essentials series.

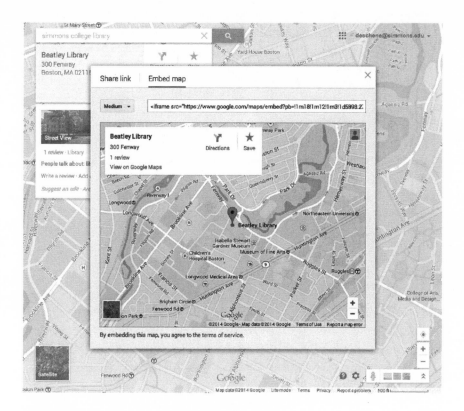

Figure 5.9. Google Maps: embed map

SHOWCASING YOUR VALUE USING A STATISTICS WEBSITE BUILT WITH SHEETSEE.JS

As part of the library community, we understand all the great things libraries do for their populations. With this project, you'll be able to easily build a data-driven website that showcases the resources and services your library provides. Using Sheetsee.js you can build an attractive data dashboard website with very little hands-on coding. You're able to display the data and automatically build a chart or graph to visualize any library data points. Sheetsee formats data tables automatically and provides options to sort and filter like a normal spreadsheet.

Although Sheetsee.js is JavaScript based, don't be afraid if you've never worked with JavaScript—there is very little actual coding from scratch. You'll need web space to host the web page you create and a

Google Drive account, but those are the only requirements. The Sheetsee.js provides great examples and in-depth documentation if you want to dive deeper into customizing the site.

Let's imagine we want to create a web page to showcase some statistics from the library's reference desk to demonstrate the value the reference desk provides to patrons. We'll work with the following statistics as an example, but feel free to substitute your own. You can add as many data points as you want.

- Total reference questions answered: 2,000
- Walk-up reference questions: 1,000
- E-mail reference questions: 500
- Telephone reference questions: 500

Setting Up and Exploring Sheetsee.js

Before creating your own Sheetsee site, it is a good idea to familiarize yourself with the examples provided in the download. There are two main pieces to set up Sheetsee.js: download the package, and upload the Sheetsee package to your web space. Here are the details for each setup step:

1. Visit https://github.com/jlord/sheetsee.js, and click the Download ZIP button on the right side of the screen. This will download all the files you need to use Sheetsee.js along with an example page you can reuse in your own project. Once you've downloaded the file, unzip it to an appropriate location on your computer.
2. Using an FTP client, such as FileZilla, upload the entire sheetsee.js-master folder to your web space. You should then be able to open a browser and navigate to [your domain]/sheetsee.js-master/ site to view the demo site.

Sheetsee works by taking the data from a Google spreadsheet and displaying it in a dynamic way. Check out [your domain]/sheetsee.js-master/site/demos/demo-table.html and [your domain]/sheetsee.js-master/site/demos/demo-chart.html to view examples of table data and chart data. From either of those pages, click the Spreadsheet link near the top of the page. This will open the Google spreadsheet used to store the data that is being displayed. For our library data website, we will need to create a similar sheet in Google.

Customizing Sheetsee.js for Your Data

Now that you've seen how Sheetsee.js presents data, you can customize it to work with your own data points. We will build a Sheetsee data table using the data points from the reference desk that were previously referred to. There are two main steps in this process: creating a Google spreadsheet to store your data points and customizing the Sheetsee.js file so it is able to talk to your spreadsheet.

The first thing you'll need to do is create a Google spreadsheet using http://drive.google.com. If you don't have a Gmail or Google Apps account, you'll need to create it via Google. Let's assume you have a Google account already. From http://drive.google.com, click the red Create button, and select Spreadsheet from the list. A new spreadsheet will open; give it a name by clicking the Untitled Spreadsheet link in the upper left corner of the screen. Then, add your data points to the sheet. Be sure to also add a header row that provides a column name (see figure 5.10). For now, let's keep things simple and use two columns: one with the name of the data point and a second containing the numeric value for the data point.

Once you have entered in your data, you will need to make sure your spreadsheet settings are configured to work with Sheetsee.js and capture the unique ID for your sheet. You will need to set your Google Spreadsheet to publish to the web, so make sure there is no sensitive data included in it. To configure the publishing settings, follow these steps:

1. In your Google Spreadsheet, navigate to File > Publish to the Web.
2. Make sure the "Automatically republish when changes are made" box is checked.
3. Click the Start Publishing button; if prompted with a "Are you sure?" message, click OK.

To get the spreadsheet's unique ID, follow these steps:

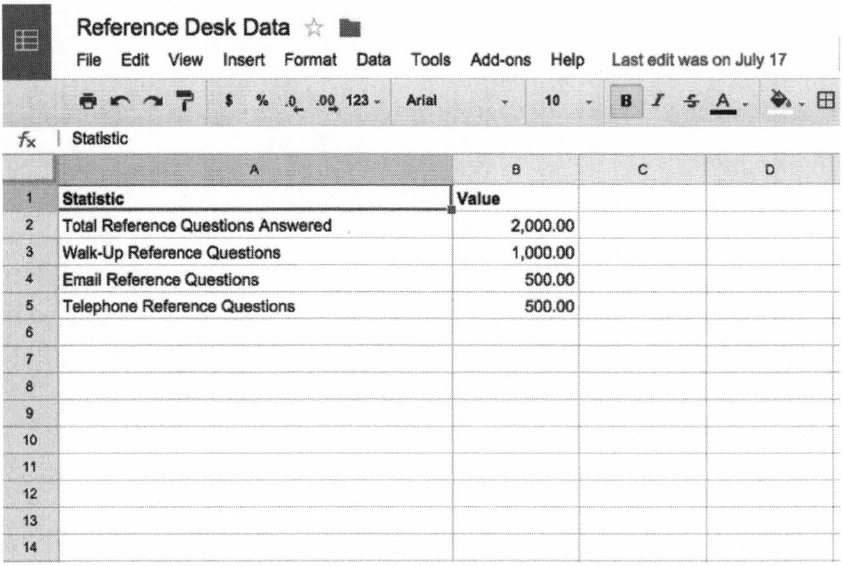

Figure 5.10.   Google Sheets: spreadsheet for Sheetsee.js

1. Navigate to your browser's address bar. The address should look something like this: https://docs.google.com/a/simmons.edu/spreadsheets/d/1GL-2xIEgA286SzoBbBj9JxXPGXbB0GUBK UHoSSv11UU/edit#gid=0.
2. Copy the unique ID from the URL. This appears toward the end of the URL. It is bolded here: https://docs.google.com/a/simmons.edu/spreadsheets/d/1GL-2xIEgA286SzoBbBj 9JxXPGXbB0GUBKUHoSSv11UU/edit#gid=0.

Creating Your Statistics Web Page

There is a simplified version of Sheetsee.js, created specifically with libraries in mind, available at https://github.com. Download these files, and upload the folder to your web space. Then navigate to [your domain]/sheetsee4lib to view the basic page and verify you can see data in the table and the chart. The example index.html page connects to the sample Google Spreadsheet listed previously above. Once you can see the example, you'll want to customize the page to pull from your own spreadsheet.

Open your favorite text editor to edit the index.html file included in the sheetsee4lib files you downloaded. Don't worry if you're a beginner at coding—we're not going to need to modify too much in order to get a working page. You need to update two pieces of the code in order to point the file to your own data.

1. Scroll all the way to the bottom of the file, and find the line starting with "var URL =". Replace the value after the equals sign with the unique ID from your own spreadsheet. Make sure you don't remove the double quotation marks around it.

2. Near the top of the HTML body tag is a link to the spreadsheet that you will need to update as well. Find the line "<p><a href="https://docs.google.com/a/github.com/spreadsheet/ccc?key=1GL-2xIEgA286SzoBbBj9JxXPGXbB0GUBKUHo SSv11UU&usp=drive_web#gid=0"target="_blank">spreadsheet </a><p>" and replace everything after "key=" but before the "&usp" with your unique ID. The part you will need to re-place is bolded above.

Return to your browser window, and refresh your [your domain]/ sheetsee4lib page. You should now see your own data populated in the table. This is a great start to building a data-driven web page, but there are many other customizations and enhancements you can do to make it even better. Using the documentation on the Sheetsee.js GitHub page, you can build other data visualizations. If you're comfortable with HTML and CSS, you can customize the layout of the page to match your organization's web page.

MANAGING MEETING SPACE WITH GOOGLE CALENDAR

Does your library oversee public meeting spaces? Controlling bookings, managing reservations, and providing room availability to the community can become an organizational challenge. However, using Google Calendar managing room reservations is much easier. With Google Calendar you can easily set up calendars to manage space bookings and inform patrons of room availability.

You might be familiar with Google Calendar for organizing your personal calendar, but you can use this tool to create calendars for each of your public, bookable spaces to simplify room management in your library. Using Google Calendar, your patrons are able to access room reservation information from anywhere and easily control what hours the rooms are available for booking. You can also create a centralized, public calendar view so patrons can see when rooms are available.

After setting up Google Calendar for your library's bookable spaces, your staff will be able to easily book rooms for patrons and patrons will be able to see when rooms are available or booked. Google Calendar provides plenty of features and is customizable so you can share as much or as little information with your community about meetings taking place in the bookable spaces. Let's have a look at setting up and managing Google Calendars for managing library room reservations.

Creating Google Calendars for Meeting Spaces

If you don't have a Google Apps account, create one via http://accounts. google.com, using the Create Account link. Once you have created an account, navigate to the Google Calendar application by visiting http:// calendar.google.com. Gather a list of all the rooms your library wants to manage bookings for, along with the details you want to include about each space (e.g., number of seats; equipment such as flat-screen projection, DVD player, white board, etc.; and location of the room). We'll use the below list as an example:

- Executive Conference Room

   12 Seats
   Flat-screen television with laptop projection

- Children's Classroom

   30 seats
   Podium with computer and projection screen

- Small Meeting Room

   8 Seats
   White board

In Google Calendar you will need to set up a calendar for each room and configure some special settings for the room calendars. Take the following steps for each room calendar you want to create:

1. In Google Calendar click the down-arrow icon next to My Calendars, and select the Create New Calendar option.
2. Fill out the calendar name, description, and location information. Include the number of seats and equipment, along with any other important details in the Description field.
3. Check the "Make this calendar public" option if you want to share the room's schedule with patrons on your website. If you want to share the free/busy information but hide the details, check the "Share only my free/busy information" checkbox.
4. Click Create Calendar. You will now see the new calendar under the list of My Calendars in Google Calendar.

Configuring Room Google Calendars

Now that you've created your calendars, you will need to adjust some settings since they are resource calendars. These are the criteria for our example rooms: these are rooms that staff may book on behalf of patrons; patrons need to be able to see when rooms are available via the website; and the rooms are available only during hours when the library is normally open. We'll need to tweak some settings in order to meet our needs for these resource calendars.

1. Mouse over the calendar you want to configure, and click the down-arrow button. Then select Calendar Settings.
2. Scroll down to the "Auto-accept invitations" area and select the "Auto-accept invitations that do not conflict" option. This will prevent the calendar from accepting invitations when there is already a meeting scheduled in the room at the selected time.
3. Navigate to the Embed This Calendar area. You will see a box with code that you can paste into your website to show the room availability to your community. If you want to change the appearance of the calendar, use the "Customize the color, size, and other options" link.
4. Click the Save button to save your selections.

Finally, to ensure no one is able to book the room calendar when the library is closed, you will need to create recurring events to "block" the time off in your calendar—one at the beginning of the day and one at the end of the day—for days you are open. On days you are closed, you will need to create a single event that blocks the entire day. Your Google Calendar is set up by default to be available from 12:00 a.m. to 11:59 p.m. Let's assume the library is open from 9:00 a.m. to 6:00 p.m., Monday through Friday, and closed on Saturdays and Sundays. We'll need to create recurring events for each scenario.

1. From the main Google Calendar page, click the red Create button.
2. Set the date to an upcoming Monday. Set the title of the event to Library Closed, and make sure the appropriate room calendar is selected from the Calendar drop-down under Event Details.
3. Set the event time for 12:00 a.m. to 9:00 a.m.
4. Check the Repeat check box. The Repeat box will open.

   a. Set the Repeats: drop down to Every Weekday (Monday to Friday)
   b. Click the Done button. The event will now repeat every weekday.

5. Select Gray as the event color, which will be a visual cue to indicate the room is unavailable during this time.
6. Click the red Save button.

You will need to complete these steps to set up recurring events that indicate the library is also closed from 6:00 p.m. to 11:59 p.m. and also a closed event for Saturdays and one for Sundays. For the Saturday and Sunday events, when creating the event, use the All Day option in the Create Event screen. When you're finished, the first calendar should resemble the example in figure 5.11.

Next, go ahead and set up calendars for any other meeting rooms in your library. Once all the calendars have been created and configured, you can begin using them to reserve meeting rooms.

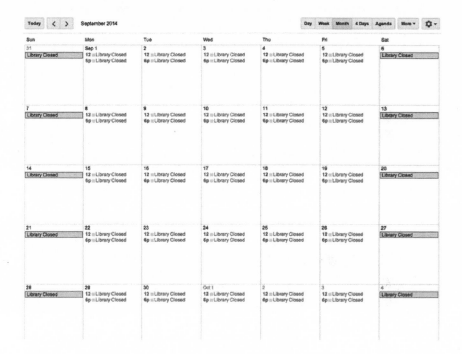

Figure 5.11.   Google Calendar: meeting room calendar

Creating Room Bookings on Google Calendar

Using the Google Calendars you've set up, patrons and staff will be able to reserve rooms when they are available either via their own Google Calendar account or by requesting the space be reserved by a library staff member. If you want to allow patrons to reserve rooms independently, you can share the calendar's e-mail address with patrons, allowing patrons to "invite" the room to their event the same way they would invite another guest. To locate the e-mail address for your calendar, navigate to the Calendar Settings page and look under the Calendar Address section. Here you will find the e-mail address for your calendar. You can provide this e-mail address to patrons to allow them to "invite" the room to their meeting. Since you have selected to "Auto-accept invitations that do not conflict," the room will be reserved automatically when someone invites it to an event, as long as it is not already reserved at that time. This approach assumes your patrons have their own Google Calendar account and your library is comfortable with unmediated booking.

If your library needs more control over room reservations, for example, if you have a high demand for meeting space, you may want to take a staff-mediated approach to booking rooms. The Google Calendar you have created for your meeting room can be used by staff only to create and edit bookings on behalf of patrons. For unmediated bookings, you will not make the room calendar's meeting address public. Instead, you'll need to share the calendar with other staff members and make sure they have edit rights so they can create and edit bookings. To share the calendar with other staff members, follow these steps:

1. Mouse over the calendar you want to configure, and click the down-arrow button. Then select Calendar Settings.
2. Navigate to the Share This Calendar page using the navigation links.
3. Enter in the e-mail addresses of the staff members you want to have access to the calendar.
4. Click the Save button.

The staff members you have invited to view and edit the calendar will receive e-mail invitations to manage the resource calendar and will be able to create events on behalf of patrons. You might consider setting up an online form (perhaps with Google Docs) where patrons can request a room be reserved for their event. You can also use the Embed This Calendar option on the Calendar Settings page to display the calendar on your website so patrons are able to see which rooms are available when before requesting a room be booked. Using Google Calendar for room management makes the entire process more streamlined, and there will be more transparency for patrons to be able to see when rooms are available.

6

TIPS AND TRICKS

Regardless of whether you implement one or all of the free technology tools discussed in this book, there are some bits of advice that apply to almost any technology initiative. The suggestions listed below are important for managing these technology solutions in the long run, getting user buy-in, and developing your own tech savviness. Follow these recommendations, and you'll be able to lead conversations about these tools and answer any questions stakeholders or potential users may have.

DETERMINE YOUR GOALS FOR A TECHNOLOGY TOOL BEFORE SELECTING AND IMPLEMENTING IT

I have been part of many successful technology implementations and others that weren't as successful. The successful technology projects (not only when using free tools) always have a clear purpose or goal in mind before the solution is determined. This can be a tricky conversation to encourage, especially when an influential member of the staff is telling everyone, "We need to use Guide on the Side! It's so cool and awesome!" (for example). Guide on the Side certainly provides fantastic, easy to use, tutorial-building functionality, but is there a need or demand for that at your library? If so, great! However, you should always consider the goals for the application before spending time or resources on implementing it.

DOCUMENT THE BUSINESS PROCESS (WHO IS RESPONSIBLE FOR DOING WHAT)

If you have decided to implement one of these tools, you'll need to determine who is going to be responsible for one or more of the following areas (depending on the type of solution it is, such as an open-source web application [e.g., CORAL] or free online tool [e.g., Google Calendar]):

- Installation of and upgrades to the software
- Managing user accounts/access
- Creating and maintaining content or data
- Assessing the usage and usefulness of the system

In your library there may be only one person responsible for all of these things, or it may be more of a team effort. It is important to be clear whether you are supporting the technology solo or if it is a shared effort. This way there is an understanding of expectations and documentation of the responsibilities associated with a certain librarian's role in case that person leaves. For example, with Google Calendar, the systems and web librarian may be responsible for managing access, while the access services librarian creates and maintains the data and the user experience librarian oversees assessing the usefulness of the tool. These three people need to work together in order for the tool to be a success.

DOCUMENT HOW YOU'RE USING THE TOOL AND WHY

The tools featured in this book provide more than adequate documentation on how to configure and use it. However, from library to library, the tools may be used in very different ways. There may be a special way to enter data or certain standards that are specific to your library. It is important to make sure you create supplemental documentation that explains how your library uses the tool and any unique elements that might not be obvious to a new staff member. For example, if you're using WordPress to manage internal announcements, you may have specific tags you want writers to apply in order to keep your content more organized and findable in WordPress. Documenting these kinds of specifics will make managing the tool much smoother.

KEEP ABREAST OF UPDATES AND FEATURES ON FREE TOOLS

Coordinating the installation and setup of a new technology is no small feat, but you can't forget about its existence once it's up and running. With certain tools, especially open-source application, it is important to figure out how to keep up to date with new releases or changes to the tool. You may be able to subscribe to a listserv, follow the software's website or blog, or join an online forum. If you stay on top of changes the developers plan to make to a new version, you can adequately plan for the changes and notify other staff members who may be impacted.

USE A PASSWORD-MANAGEMENT TOOL TO KEEP TRACK OF USERNAMES AND PASSWORDS

Even if you don't plan on implementing any of the tools discussed in this book, I still recommend using a password manager to manage your user accounts. This can be especially helpful if you have shared accounts that multiple staff members use. A password manager is a small database that allows you to create a secure file containing all of your usernames and passwords. You use one master password to unlock the database. You can easily search the database, edit entries, and often autogenerate secure passwords (if you're tired of having to come up with them yourself). One of the most popular free tools for this is KeePass (http://keepass.info), which is available for PC and Mac.

LEARN HOW TO USE WEB-DEVELOPER TOOLS

If you do any kind of web development, design, or editing, learning the ins and outs of the browser's web-developer tools is a fantastic skill to invest time in. It will make your website coding projects much easier! Most modern browsers come with these web-developer tools built in.

You may be familiar with Firebug, a Firefox extension that allows you to inspect your web code and modify the markup in real time. The Google Chrome browser has an equivalent set of tools built in to the browser called Developer Tools. These can be launched by right-clicking anywhere on a web page and selecting Inspect Element. A window will pop up on the bottom of your browser window, and you will be able to dive into the markup to see how something is styled on the page. You can learn more details about these DevTools by visiting https://developer.chrome.com/devtools.

Figure 6.1.　Google Chrome: web-developer tools

BECOME FAMILIAR WITH VERSION CONTROL

Version control is a method of saving various versions of files over time, so you can easily revert back to a former version of a file when necessary. For example, if you're managing a set of HTML and CSS files for a website, you would keep a copy of each version of each file, before making changes, instead of overwriting the file. If you are concurrently editing web files with a team of people, there is version-control software that can assist in merging files changed by multiple people. If you work solo or on a small, two- to three-person team, you might be able to come up with a simple version-control process without implementing software, but if you are working with a larger team, consider using a software such as Git or Subversion to manage version control.

Both Git and Subversion are available for free to download. In this book, and in the majority of open-source library projects I've come across, Git seems a popular choice. Tools I've mentioned such as Guide on the Side, CORAL, and Sheetsee.js all use GitHub to host their code. GitHub is the place where these open-source tools store their code, and Git is the version-control software they're using to manage changes. Find out more about Git at http://git-scm.com, an online e-book all about the version-control software.

CONSIDER YOUR CONTENT/DATA MANAGEMENT STRATEGY

Whichever tool you implement, you need to make sure you have a strategy for taking regular backups of your data (if you're using an open-source application that uses a database, such as CORAL or WordPress). There are tools you can use to automate these data backups such as phpMyBackupPro (www.phpmybackuppro.net). It is also important to have a plan in case you ever need to migrate your data to a different system (yes, you need to consider that one day this awesome new tech tool might become obsolete). When considering different tools, think about how you might go about taking your data with you.

Many tools have some kind of data-export option that will export your data in a CSV or Excel file. If you're using a MySQL database-based application, you can use the mysqldump function to export your data to a local file. This may not seem like an exciting task, because it's so theoretical at the time of implementing a new tool, but it is important to consider what your "exit strategy" might be from this tool in the future. If a tool doesn't allow you to export your data or provide an off-line way to save something, consider if you're okay taking the risk of losing your content if the tool becomes obsolete or moves to a paid model in the future.

7

FUTURE TRENDS

One of the only things we know for certain about technology is that it will continue to evolve over time. Change is a constant in the world of technology, and you need to be mindful of it in order to have success using the free tools in this book or any with technology initiative. You'll need to be flexible and comfortable with a small amount of risk using these free tools. Even if they one day become paid tools or disappear completely (remember the retirement of Google Reader in 2013), there will be alternatives. This is another reason it's important to focus any technology selection and implementation on your goals and purpose, instead of on the tool itself.

In addition to the changes that might occur to a technology solution you've adopted, you also need to be aware of when an application no longer meets the needs of your users, because your users' needs have changed. Consider the still-changing evolution of online searching in libraries. First came the online catalog, in lieu of the card catalog, which enabled patrons to search the library's collection from their computer. This eventually evolved into federated searching, the ability to send a single query to multiple databases, and often sort or limit using facets. Currently, discovery services are the "hot" technology in library search-ing, facilitating a single database containing the majority of library col-lections, both online and physical, in a single database. In this example, both the technology and patron needs were evolving in tandem. Users became accustomed to using search interfaces like those provided by

Google and Amazon. Their expectations were that the library would provide the same easy-to-use search interface for library resources.

The searching example described above also points to another important point: you have to stay on top of the evolution of technology, both inside and outside of libraries, in order to not be blindsided by the emergence of new technology. If you're not following tech blogs, regularly reading articles from authoritative sources, and networking with other technology professionals, start now! And if you need some source suggestions, check out the recommended reading section that follows.

RECOMMENDED READING

PRINT RESOURCES

Burke, John. 2013. *Neal-Schuman Library Technology Companion: A Basic Guide for Library Staff.* Chicago: American Library Association. A great resource for learning the basics and history of technology in libraries. Perfect for library science students or those new to the profession.

Clark, Larra, and Denise Davis. 2009. *The State of Funding for Library Technology in Today's Economy.* Library Technology Reports. Chicago: American Library Association. Analysis of a major survey on library technology funding and trends in how libraries are paying for technology projects. Includes a chapter on "Doing More with Less."

Pogue, David. 2014. *Pogue's Basics: Essential Tips and Shortcuts (That No One Bothers to Tell You) for Simplifying the Technology in Your Life.* New York: Flatiron Books. David Pogue is a prolific consumer technology writer. In this book, he discusses great everyday tips and tricks to help you learn more about the technology in your work and personal life.

Shirky, Clay. 2009. *Here Comes Everybody: The Power of Organizing without Organizations.* New York: Penguin. Gives you the "big picture" about how technology is transforming the human race, especially our ability to collaborate and build relationships on a global scale.

Varnum, Kenneth K. 2014. *The Top Technologies Every Librarian Needs to Know: A LITA Guide.* Chicago: American Library Association. Need help figuring out where to spend your time and money for the greatest benefits? This book helps you understand technology trends and determine what might work best for your library.

TECHNOLOGY BLOGS

(For library-specific blogs, refer to chapter 2.)

Mashable | http://mashable.com. A fantastic website if you're looking for a site that gives you every single piece of technology-related news all in one place.

Bits from the *New York Times* | http://bits.blogs.nytimes.com. A great blog on the latest technology news, with unbiased reporting from the *New York Times*.

ReadWriteWeb | http://readwrite.com. This site features articles about web technologies from coding hacks to consumer technology reviews.

TechCrunch | http://techcrunch.com. The latest technology news, with a focus on start-ups and emerging trends.

INDEX

ABOUT THE AUTHOR

Amy Deschenes specializes in making the library more user-friendly. She has worked in libraries since 2009 and is currently the library user experience specialist at Harvard University. Prior to her current role, she worked on leading technology projects as the systems and web applications librarian at Simmons College Library. There, she built responsive websites, implemented countless open-source apps, organized the library's benchmarking statistics, and performed usability testing—all without spending a dime of the library's budget. She is an advocate for thoughtful adoption of technology solutions and always considering the user's needs.

Amy delights in leading teams to discover how libraries can make the best use of technology and exceed user expectations. She also enjoys encouraging students and peers to experiment and evaluate free technology solutions. So be brave, and try at least one of the tools in this book! If you have any questions, she can be reached via Twitter @amyhannah.